# I'M A TEACHER,
# GET ME OUT OF HERE!

Characters referred to in this book are composite characters and essentially interventions of my own, although everything that happens is based on real incidents.

# I'M A TEACHER,
# GET ME OUT OF HERE!

## Francis Gilbert

✳ SHORT BOOKS

This paperback edition first published in 2005 by
Short Books
15 Highbury Terrace
London N5 1UP

10 9 8 7 6 5 4 3 2 1
Copyright ©
Francis Gilbert 2004

A CIP catalogue record for this book
is available from the British Library.

ISBN 1-904977-02-2

Printed by Bookmarque Ltd, Croydon, Surrey

For every teacher who doesn't want to get up in the morning

To Erica & Theo - the heart of everything

In memory of Ruth and Cecil Gilbert,
the best teachers I ever had

# PART ONE

## 'I AIN'T DONE NUFFINK WRONG'

The professor's bloodshot eyes scanned the candidates. He leaned towards me. I could smell the whisky on his breath, I could see bits of grey stubble sneaking out of his red cheeks, I could feel his frustration. He continued in his inimitable, rasping fashion: "So you're telling me that none of you know what you would do if one of your pupils wrote, 'I ain't done nuffink wrong'?"

There was another tense silence. We shifted uneasily in our seats. All of us were at an interview that could possibly shape the rest of our lives. I had failed to get on any of the other teacher-training courses I had applied for because I had been far too bolshy and, though I would have normally voiced my views without a second thought, I drew breath here. In my estimation of things, a year of doing crappy, menial jobs in Brighton beckoned if I didn't get on this course.

Eventually, Veronica, a girl with tasteful gold earrings and dressed in a very expensive grey cardigan, spoke up in a clipped Cheltenham Ladies' College accent: "I would mark such a candidate as being incorrect in his usage of the English language."

Professor Holmes appeared to nod at this but I could see that his ever-so-slightly trembling fingers were bunched into fists. Soon every other interviewee, who was grouped around the square table in the bleak, strip-lit room, had joined in: such a candidate had obviously failed to write English correctly and needed to be informed of this.

Holmes sighed and responded, "But are none of you aware that Standard English was invented in the late eighteenth century by grammarians who wanted to subjugate the working classes and kill off their dialects?"

A tremor swept through the candidates. They were all conscious that they had said the wrong thing. Oh no! Catastrophe! The goody-goodies had got it wrong. I laughed. I couldn't believe it. Contrary to all expectations I had stumbled across a professor who had similar views to mine.

Now to understand who I was back in 1989 and why I responded so enthusiastically to Holmes's statement, you need to consider my dress and haircut. I had long, greasy red hair that was tied back in a ponytail and hung limply around my waist, I was wearing my best Paisley shirt that was studded intermittently with little pinhole burns acquired during some all-night bender, my bomber jacket was ripped and the orange lining was turning black and my jeans and desert boots were both knackered.

I was, in short, a hippy who had arrived on the planet twenty years too late. I had flourished at Sussex University doing an English degree because this radical university had nurtured my revolutionary spirit, encouraged me to read William Blake and John Milton and had allowed me space to smoke dandelion cigarettes and discuss changing the world. But the trouble was that the rest of the world wasn't like Sussex. It was mean and cruel and capitalist. I knew that I wouldn't get far declaiming Blake in darkened, coughing basement flats and attempting to write agit-prop plays. I knew that I had to get a job.

Teaching English was the only thing that remotely

appealed. I would be able to teach Blake to working-class kids and liberate them from their mind-forged manacles. However, I had been sorely disappointed when I had been interviewed at various teacher-training institutions round the country. None of the teacher trainers had been impressed by my ideas of teaching Ian McEwan's *The Cement Garden* (a novel about masturbation, murder and incest) to teenagers or fostering their poetic spirits with Philip Larkin's *This Be The Verse* ("They fuck you up your mum and dad..."). I had been turned down for every institution.

Until Holmes. He was a kindred spirit. As the ever-so-well-behaved candidates in their suits and frocks reeled from being admonished by him, I launched into a tirade against the prescriptive grammarians who had used the English language to humiliate the masses.

"We shouldn't be marking such a pupil as wrong. That would be to kill off the pupil's spirit. We need to make such pupils proud of their local dialects, to celebrate them. For the last hundred years we have used education to crush the natural vigour of such dialects but this isn't education, this is indoctrination," I said in such an animated fashion that my John Lennon wire spectacles nearly fell off my nose.

Holmes clapped his hands together, little bits of saliva sprayed out of his mouth as he voiced his approbation for my point. "I couldn't agree more," he spluttered. Soon, everyone else was echoing my views around the conference table. Yes, pupils' non-standard usage of the English language must be celebrated, they all said.

At the end of my individual interview with Holmes he let it be known that I had got a place on the Post-Graduate Course in Education to teach Secondary English at the Faculty for Child-Learning at Cambridge University. He told me that I should on no account cut my hair, that I should continue to fight the good fight and that my dress was entirely appropriate.

I was very happy. I would have a full grant, a nice place to stay amidst the Gothic colleges and I could feel that my revolutionary credentials were still intact.

## A PRIMARY EDUCATION

Paul Travis quivered with indignation and shouted. "Can you believe that they said that to me? Can you believe that?"

I shook my head. I was standing in a primary school

classroom which had no walls; I could see just about every class in the whole school going about its business. The noise was deafening and the vision before me was a benign version of a Bruegel depiction of Hell.

Children were prodding each other with tongs, pulling each other's hair, throwing plasticine at the windows, tipping water on the floor, playing football with wooden blocks, scribbling on each other's faces and tugging on all the female teachers' skirts. The only teacher who was unmolested was Paul Travis, a diminutive man with a trim beard, a Cornish brogue and a six-foot wife. He had told me about his wife the moment I stepped foot into the primary school where I was supposed to do a couple of weeks observation before starting my teacher-training course.

Now he was informing me why he had been turned down for the post of Deputy Head at the school.

"Because I don't have any children! That's what they asked me about repeatedly in the interview. Why didn't I have any children? They didn't bother with asking whether I was a good teacher or not. No. They just wanted to hear about my marriage. Well, as you can imagine, I gave them a piece of my mind. I told the governors that they could stuff their job."

At the time I didn't realise the full implications of

what Travis was saying, but I do now. Because he was an odd-looking man with a great, strapping, moustached German wife (I saw her dropping him off in the mornings) and teaching in the primary sector, which is largely staffed by middle-aged housewives, the powers-that-be assumed he was a pervert. He was unlucky; teaching at a time when men were not encouraged to teach younger children.

This was a shame because he was a good teacher. He was the only pedagogue who taught his pupils the basics: mental arithmetic, reading and writing. Again, he was a few years ahead of his time. His ideas about numeracy and literacy were to become orthodoxy by the time he retired, but not during his tenure.

My experience observing him made me realise that I had made the right decision in opting to teach in the secondary sector; the male species was not welcome in the world of primary.

## THE COURSE BEGINS AND
## THE BERLIN WALL CRUMBLES

I started my course at Cambridge in October of 1989 with such high hopes. I had been born in Cambridge and lived there until I was six when we moved to London. I remembered happy times when my father used to take us to the park and I would play on the swings, the roundabout and rush around in the paddling pool.

I was still partly in love with the beauty of the town: the gorgeous lawns, the mystical quads, the punts on the river, the Gothic brilliancies of King's College, the sun-dappled bridges and tree-lined avenues made me feel as if I was living in my own modern-day fairytale. It was a Marxist fairytale, but a fairytale nevertheless, because it was here that I planned to gather all the intellectual and emotional resources to enable me to venture forth into the dark forest of working class Britain where I would slay the dragons of class envy and alienation. Even then I realised that this was a preposterously ambitious task but I felt somehow, with the help of Holmes, I might be able to achieve something important.

\*\*\*

So you can imagine my disappointment when nothing quite turned out as I had planned. Instead of a lovely snug nook in a Cambridge college, I was asked to stay in a horrible room in a converted army barracks on the edge of town. Instead of luxuriating in the brilliant beauty of the town, I came to feel that it masked a very ugly complacency. Instead of finding an important ally in Holmes, I found an outright enemy.

As students we were expected to attend lectures from nine to five at the Faculty for Child-Learning in Oboe Street. Most of these lectures were given by Holmes. In them he espoused the causes of child-centred learning. Teachers should never lecture but always make children experience learning. The teacher wasn't the expert, the pedagogue or the leader, he was merely the facilitator. Pupils should discover things for themselves in groups. I had seen the hellish consequences of such an approach to teaching in my primary school observation and was naturally suspicious of this philosophy. I was particularly dubious about it when Holmes espoused its virtues because he rarely practised what he preached: we were forced to listen to his slurping, spitting lectures all day in silence.

But I didn't say anything until the day after the Berlin Wall came down. It was a mild November day; golden, curled leaves drifted off the bleak trees in Oboe Street. I suppose something in me realised that day that the game was up regarding the Revolution. I saw that it was never going to happen and this made me feel the whole of Holmes's philosophy was a sham.

He seemed upset. After lunch, his words were even more slurred and spluttery than normal but I was ruthless. When he started saying yet again that children should learn the values of co-operation and equality by working in non-hierarchical groups, I put my hand up and asked why he wasn't putting us into groups so that we could form our own views about his teaching. There was a quiet murmur of concurrence from the students.

Holmes reddened even more than usual and said that of course all that stuff would be happening in due course.

"But when, when, Professor Holmes? We've been sitting here for weeks listening to your interminable lectures and we're sick of it. We've had enough," I proclaimed angrily. Holmes knew he was in a spot of bother and squirmed in his seat. He reached into the pocket of his oatmeal jacket and produced a gold watch. He looked at it as he said, "Who? Who are all these people? Maybe they should put their hands up. I'm a democrat at heart, you know, and welcome any voice from the masses."

No one except me put their hands up, although I

knew that nearly everyone else felt the same way as I did.

After the session, Holmes called me over to see him. I thought for a moment that it might have been to make some kind of peace with me. Having now taught many difficult pupils, I now know that I wasn't that difficult. I was willing to listen, to concede defeat if I was given the right reasons. But Holmes squared up to me. He jabbed a trembling finger at me. The smell of whisky flooded around my face as he said, "You'd better watch out, Gilbert. You're heading to fail this course. I can really see you failing this course."

*\*\**

The next day, feeling depressed, I walked out on to the rain-slicked streets of Cambridge and wandered about the town, ruminating upon my wretched situation. Holmes wanted to fail me, no one else on the course really wanted to talk to me and I had no idea what I wanted to do with my life apart from teaching. Added to which I was finding the environment, the physical and emotional environment of Cambridge, really oppressive. As I walked past my childhood home in Station Avenue I remembered the bitter divorce of my parents.

I am five years old. I am crying on the stairs of that house. There are screams upstairs. My father's husky shouts. "Let me in this room. Let me in this room."

"Go away. Get away from me!" my mother screams.

Another snapshot. My father is crying this time. He has locked himself in the bathroom. "What's the matter with Daddy?" I ask my mother. She shrugs callously, "He's just crying like a baby... because he is a baby."

I didn't want to think about it. I knew that, deep down, here was the reason I wanted to be a teacher but I wouldn't admit it. I wanted to be a parent to troubled children. To treat them better than my parents had treated me, to give them love and attention and patience, not recriminations and pain.

Yet more echoes flittered through my mind as I ran away from the neat gardens and book-lined drawing rooms of Station Avenue. My father is dropping me off at school. For some reason, I start to cry as I say goodbye to him.

"I'm going away now Francis. I'm going away for quite a while, but you'll like it here," he says. "I am going away to this place called America. You won't see me for a while."

# FIRST VISIONS OF COVENTRY

Veronica shrank back in horror as a huge black kid in a torn leather jacket lurched back in his chair away from his computer screen and flicked some ash over his shoulder.

"Oh no, Francis, I can't teach here," she said, feeling her pearly necklace with panicky fingers. "That boy is openly smoking in front of his teacher!"

I shrugged. It all looked rather intriguing to me. Having spent a term listening to interminable lectures and paying the odd visit to well-behaved schools in the leafy environs of Cambridge and Peterborough, I had begun to be heartily sick of ordinary schools.

This school situated in the sordid depths of a council estate on the edge of Coventry was different. I knew that Holmes thought that it would defeat me and would ensure I definitely fail the course, but wandering around the corridors I was beginning to warm to it. It was the only school where the kids hadn't stared at me for having long, greasy hair for a start. None of the teachers had asked me to wear a tie the next time I visited.

I laughed as the black kid offered me a cigarette, crouched down beside him and asked him what he was up to. "Just trying to get this 'puter to work," he said mournfully.

"Perhaps, you'd better try the 'on' button," I replied, pushing the relevant button and watching the kid's amazement as the machine sprang into life. He clapped his hands and whooped, "Hey that's good man, that's good!"

At that moment Jesse Stevens, the Head of English who was in charge of the class, walked up beside me and patted my back. The rest of the student teachers were cowering in a corner, not quite knowing what to do with themselves – but I felt at home here.

Jesse fluttered his eyelashes. They were caked in black eye-liner. His tired face brightened into a smile. "You seem to be very technically minded," he said to me without a trace of irony. His nose, his cheeks and eyes were sheened with the Acorn Start Up Screen. His earring glinted in the ghostly glow. His glittering features seemed like a good omen.

Every other student tried to dodge out of being sent to Coventry when we got back to Cambridge. No one wanted to be part of Jesse Stevens's department, even if it was only for a term. Holmes was disappointed in them but let them go to suitably easy schools in Cambridge and Peterborough. Only a handful of students opted to go to schools in Coventry and most of these were placed in nice-ish establishments in the centre of the town. Only Holmes's two *bêtes noires* got to go to Oakway Grove where Jesse taught – me and a slobbish character called Keith who specialised in heavy metal music, blowing his nose into soiled handkerchiefs and turning up late to lectures.

The idea of the course was that we would absorb the theory in the first term, teach in a school in the second, and reflect and write up what had happened in the third. The teaching placement was by far the most important part of the course; students were expected to teach more or less full-time for a whole term and were observed by a mentor, a teacher at their chosen school, and assessed by the dreaded Holmes.

Before I left Holmes smiled malevolently and chuckled, "You'll like it with Jesse. I think he's your type."

## JANUARY 1990

The bald Deputy Head, Arthur Digby, threw all his school papers on the passenger seat of his Fiesta into the back and told me to sit down. He was going to give me a tour of the neighbourhood before I started teaching at Oakway Grove. He rubbed his eyes.

"I've got this terrible headache. I just don't seem to be able to get rid of it," he said, as he started up the car and we chugged around the bleak roads. It was a raw January morning; a thin drizzle descended as we ventured into the dark heart of the Oakway estate. Litter strewed the streets, everywhere there seemed to be boarded-up blocks of flats, burnt-out cars, shuttered shops, youths hanging about on corners smoking, bust-up playgrounds and endless rows of small, dreary council maisonettes that all looked exactly the same. Even the tower blocks didn't have the distinction of being big. Arthur explained that since they had closed down the car factories lots of people were without work or money. Our job was to give their offspring some kind of hope.

"It's very easy to get lost here," Arthur said, "Because everything looks the bloody same."

We got lost. Arthur didn't seem to mind. After driving around fruitlessly for half an hour, he stopped the car and rubbed his eyes.

"It's doesn't matter. You're not teaching today, are you?"

I said that I was supposed to be observing lessons.

"You're with Jesse, aren't you?" Arthur mused. "Yes, Jesse is a great chap. Although I have to say, it's all a bit awkward at the school, considering what went on before he came here. Not that the kids mind. It's only the staff he has a problem with."

I tried to press Arthur about what he meant here but he wouldn't say anymore.

## JESSE'S LESSONS

"Now children, if you think that everyone with AIDS should not be allowed to have jobs or come to school, could you walk over to the far corner of the room where I have written 'STRONGLY AGREE' and if you think differently, walk over to 'STRONGLY DISAGREE'. Right. Off we go!"

Jesse took a clog off his foot and bashed the table with it to mark the point when the pupils should start moving. I was quite surprised to see that only two children went into the STRONGLY AGREE corner and that the rest sauntered into the other corner. However, one of the kids in the STRONGLY AGREE corner seemed belligerent and the atmosphere in the classroom grew tense as Jesse questioned him as to why he had stood here.

"Well, they're all poofs that have got it and I don't think that poofs should be allowed here," he said, fixing his eyes upon Jesse.

There was a sudden uproar. The kids at the other end of the classroom started shouting at this boy, who was called Daryl Jones, "Don't say that, you sucker!"

Daryl Jones responded by hurling some abuse back at the girls who were voicing their concerns, "Fag hags! Faggy fag hags!"

Jesse waved his wrists in the air and said, "Now, now, Daryl, we all know that you have these views and we all know that I am gay, so some people might take offence at your remarks."

Daryl didn't say anything more and, miraculously, the commotion died down. The kids sat down at their desks and examined the newspaper article about people living with AIDS that Jesse handed out. I admired Jesse's courage and the way in which he seemed to have enabled the kids to have such enlightened views about sexuality. It was clear to me that he had done a lot of work with them on this topic and that he had, for the most part, probably converted them to the cause.

Jesse was a rebel. Technically, what he was doing could be construed as being illegal because the government had just passed a law that outlawed "the promotion of homosexuality".

***

As I observed more lessons I became aware that Jesse was exhausting himself. He always had to do things differently. Whereas the other English teachers would plod somewhat mechanically through a textbook, shout at pupils if they misbehaved and be thoroughly conventional in their talk, Jesse encouraged the kids to make their own films, to discuss controversial topics and to do anything but sit down and read and write. It was hard work, made even harder because the pupils were aware that he was a "soft" touch; they ate sweets in his lesson, swore regularly, had little toy fights and verbal slanging matches. Such behaviour wasn't tolerated in other lessons.

***

One day, during my second week at Oakway Grove, I found Jesse with his head in his hands. He looked like he had been crying. I asked him what the matter was. He said it was nothing; he'd been burgled quite a lot before but this time it had got to him. His boyfriend Fred had shouted at the police for not doing anything and one of the coppers had made some homophobic remark.

The next day Jesse phoned in sick. The school didn't have enough staff to cover him properly. Arthur, the Deputy Head, called Keith and me into his office. Piles of memos were stacked up so high on his desk that his tufted bald head scarcely protruded over them; he had arranged all the bumf in nice, neat squares tied together with string like bundles of wheat. He swallowed an aspirin and told me that he wanted us to take Jesse's exam classes.

"It's his wife, you know. She haunts him here. Before he came out about being gay, his wife used to teach here. She's left now, of course, but I think he finds it very strange. Her ghost haunts the corridors for him," Arthur said.

As Keith and I left Arthur's office, both of us laughed nervously. Keith wiped his sweaty hands against his *Whitesnake* T-shirt and then blew his nose. "I think that Arthur must have figured that we look like tough guys. He wouldn't have given us Jesse's classes otherwise, would he?"

"I don't know," I replied.

"None of those kids are going to fuck me around," Keith said, bunching his hands into fists and bashing them into the air.

"I'm going to teach!" he proclaimed like a gunslinger who had just determined that he was going to kick butt in Dodge City. He swaggered down the hall leaving me to my own thoughts.

I felt as if I had stepped into a strange time portal. Suddenly, from being just an ordinary student teacher wandering around a bleak comprehensive, I had entered a different dimension; a domain where I was not only responsible for the welfare of nearly a hundred children but also for an ailing teacher. The walls and floor of the school shimmered around me. I blinked. There was a tight knot of pain in my throat. I was frightened and sad and exhilarated all at the same time. For the first time in my life I felt needed, really needed. Jesse needed me, Arthur needed me, those kids needed me.

I had crossed a threshold and, like Dr Who stepping out of his Tardis, found myself in a bizarre new land. Whereas before I hadn't really noticed the noises and smells of the school except as irritations and curiosities, now they were loaded with meaning. Was that one of my classes scraping their chairs across the floors like that? What class was listening to Mozart in the far corner of the building? Should I play my classes music? Where did that smell of old socks and chewing-gum and custard come from? What would my classes smell like? Who had scribbled "I hate wankers" by the radiator next to my classroom? What graffiti would be written about me?

And beyond all of these stinks and screechings and scrapings I thought I could see the ghost of Jesse Stevens's wife walking down the corridor. She was wearing a simple floral dress and her eyes were edged with tears. What had happened to her? Was she dead? Had she died of AIDS? Crazy thoughts ran through my mind as I walked, like a condemned prisoner to the gallows, towards...

## MY FIRST EVER LESSON

This was Jesse's GCSE English class, the one which he had read articles about AIDS with, the class with the benighted, homophobic Daryl Jones. I was supposed to have another teacher in the class with me but Arthur hadn't arranged this. I was entirely on my own. I knew from observing a couple of other GCSE classes that everyone else in the English Department was reading *A Taste Of Honey* by Shelagh Delaney and asking them to do a piece of coursework on it. The play was a bleak kitchen-sink drama written in the 1960s about a moaning teenage girl living in the poverty-stricken North who sleeps with a black man and gets pregnant. I liked the text although I was aware that it was very dated in its references. However, I hadn't had any time to prepare to teach it or even to think about whether I should teach it or not; it was the only suitable book I had seen in the stock cupboard and I pulled it out without a second thought.

Without any more ado, I handed out *A Taste Of Honey*. Jesse's "fag hags", a group of pleasant girls with frizzy dyed blond hair and dressed in cheap pink and white shell suits, questioned me about what was going on.

"Where's Mr Stevens?" they asked.

"He's ill. Not here today," I said somewhat apologetically.

The girls nodded. Clearly they were used to such absences. "So what's happening, are you taking us from now on?"

"Maybe," I said hesitantly. I didn't want to hear

them moaning about me, so I hedged my bets about telling them that as far as I was concerned I had them for the rest of the term.

"Now then," I said. "Could we have quiet please? I need to see who is reading what role in this play. Could you put your hand up if you want to read?"

Everyone started shouting out that they wanted a role and then when I said they had a part they refused to take it. After ten minutes of trying to allocate roles, no one had a part. I remember feeling a sense of rising panic. What was I supposed to do? I was banking on reading the play for part of the lesson and then setting a written exercise, where they predicted what happened next, for the remainder of the lesson. But they hadn't read anything; how could they make a prediction from nothing?

These kids were laughing and jeering at me. I felt very vulnerable with my long ponytail. Sweat was beginning to seep through my shirt. I wandered around the class, trying to encourage kids on a one-to-one basis to take on a role. This worked a bit better because I managed to get a few of them to agree to read out aloud.

I succeeded in getting the play started with these readers. However, their faltering voices were virtually drowned out by the other kids who were still chatting very loudly. In particular, there was one kid, the surly, sunken-eyed Daryl Jones, who was pushing and shouting at the boy sitting next to him. He was by far the worst behaved and noisiest kid in the class. I decided that I had to take him on if I was going to get anywhere. I wasn't going to wave my wrists limply at him or do my best to ignore him, as Jesse had done; I was going to confront him. I was a tough guy. I asked him to be quiet and to listen. He didn't respond – or rather he did by shoving his friend so hard that he fell off his seat. Everyone burst out laughing. As his friend picked himself off the floor, I approached Daryl Jones.

For the first time in the lesson, everyone was quiet. All eyes swivelled round to watch me as I stalked with a red and seething face towards Jones. He grinned at everyone and then let his head flop on to the desk with a soft thud. He appeared to shut his eyes.

I didn't know what to say to him because he wasn't being noisy any more. I picked up his book which had fallen on the floor and put it beside his tousled black hair; his face was still buried in the desk.

"You have to follow this," I said in an angry but calmish voice, as I pointed at a forlorn, dog-eared page of *A Taste Of Honey*.

Jones didn't reply.

"Did you hear me?" I said.

Jones groaned in a pseudo-sleepy voice, "What, what you say?"

The class tittered. They were still watching with avid attention.

"I said you need to follow this."

"Oh, fuck off, sir," said Jones, lifting his head slightly to show his hooded eyes. "I'm just trying to have a kip here."

There was an intake of breath and then an explosion of laughter from the class. I had been humiliated. This oily little runt had humiliated me. And I felt powerless. There was nothing that I could do.

I soldiered on with the lesson. I backed away from Jones, leaving him slumped on the desk and, after the laughter had simmered down, carried on asking the few who wanted to read to read. And they did. I got to the end of the lesson. Jones didn't say another word but continued kipping. I left him well alone.

Although it wasn't a very pleasant experience, after I had recovered from my initial feelings of humiliation I began to reflect that it was all rather interesting.

Jones, for all his bolshiness, had been respectful. He'd said, "Fuck off, *sir*". His curious mixture of rebelliousness and servility struck me as odd but peculiarly comforting. I don't think anyone else in any other profession quite gets a rebuff like that; doctors, policemen, lawyers, civil servants are probably just told to fuck off, if at all. There was an aspect of gratitude and respect in Jones's insult which indicated that even when pupils are really wanting to make a teacher look like an idiot, they always have a degree of admiration for what they are trying to do.

## GHOST-BUSTING

I didn't tell anyone about what had happened with Daryl Jones. I was too ashamed. Somehow I felt that it was my fault and somehow I felt that I had dealt with him properly. However, his ghost stalked not just the lessons he was in, but others as well; the memory of that humiliation made me draw back from open confrontation unless I was certain that I could win.

I realised that schools are really the most haunted institutions in the land. While I was teaching Jesse's classes I could feel his ghost hovering over me. Pupils would turn to me and say that Mr Stevens never asked them to write essays or read silently; he did fun things.

Jesse's spirit had invaded their minds and made them mournful for the past. This in turn made me realise that ultimately their knowledge of all the teachers they had ever had must inform their judgements of me. Perhaps Jesse's wife had taught them?

I felt like a member of the Ghostbusters team – I had to destroy all of these spirits in my mind in order to become a functioning teacher. I had to bludgeon all the memories I had of my teachers so I wouldn't be endlessly judging myself against them, I had to splat the thought that I was nowhere near as charismatic as Jesse, that I didn't have the discipline of the really good teachers I had observed, that I wasn't as well informed about the National Curriculum as Veronica and the other dutiful students. I had to hose down my worries and just focus upon what the kids were learning, and not be bothered about how I appeared to them.

## SICK

At the end of the week, Arthur called Keith and me back into his office. He looked terrible. There were deep pools of blackness underneath his eyes and the sheaves of paper that had been so neatly bundled at the beginning of the week were beginning to sag. He took a deep breath and said, "Look, I have got to be honest with you, it looks like Jesse isn't going to come back this term so things will most probably carry on as they are."

Keith wrinkled his lip. He didn't look too well himself. His forehead was slicked with sweat. "So are you telling us that we have to carry on teaching those classes without any help?" he said.

Arthur nodded. "If you would. I know Francis has been doing well with Jesse's GCSE class and you are beginning to get to know Jesse's lower-school classes."

"Beginning to get to know them! You could say that!" Keith exclaimed. "I'm beginning to get to know them so well already that I am waking up in the middle of the night grinding my teeth."

Arthur sighed. "I'm sorry to hear that. I would really like to help you, Keith, the only trouble is that I myself have to go into hospital next week. It looks like I might have a tumour on my brain."

This shut Keith up. His mouth dropped open, revealing all his ground-down teeth. Both of us stared at Arthur. I said that I was very sorry to hear this. Here was another ghost in the making. I felt in my heart of hearts that Arthur was dying. Christ, what had Oakway Grove done to him?

Keith and I trooped out of the office in silence and walked down the stairs. Outside the staffroom Keith reached for his handkerchief and said, "I don't know about you but I want to get out of here alive. I'm baling out. My classes are up the wall. I hate my lodgings. I'm missing my girlfriend. The two people who are supposed to be helping us look like they are dying. It's time to jump ship!"

I shook my head. "I like it here," I said. "I'm going to stay."

Before we could talk any more an English teacher, Vivien Brand, ran out of the staffroom door and pushed through the school exit doors. We went into the staffroom and asked the last remaining English teacher, Cynthia James, what was going on. Cynthia shrugged her shoulders and said that Vivien was suffering from terrible cystitis and had decided to go home.

A few days later Vivien returned to school feeling better. Keith had been lodging with her but since the day that Arthur had informed us about the brain tumour, he hadn't returned to school and hadn't even returned to his "hateful" lodgings − apparently, he hadn't enjoyed having Vivien's teenage children thumping around all night.

When Vivien came into the staffroom, she was carrying a large, battered cardboard box. She made a beeline for me. Her nostrils were flared; something smelt really bad in that box. It turned out it contained Keith's stuff. She wanted me to return it to him when I saw him back in Cambridge. It was full of smelly socks and a stack of pornographic magazines.

Keith was quite grateful to get it back the next term. He had decided to drop off the course for the teaching practice, he said, but complete terms one and three like everyone else; he would do his teaching practice somewhere else in September.

## SKANKING AND MOOCHING

I thrived on the extra responsibility. I really liked the feeling that I mattered, that without me these kids wouldn't be getting an education. And so I made a real effort. And I found out that I enjoyed it. I liked cycling Herzog, my red mountain bike, through smoky, desolate council estates at dawn and entering the prison-like precincts of the school and delivering lessons in low-ceilinged classrooms that overlooked a raging motorway. I had never experienced a world like this before; I had gone to an undistinguished public school in east London and really only known a world of material privilege and uptight, suspicious people.

The staff and pupils at Oakway Grove weren't like that at all; nearly all the kids were from homes where both parents were unemployed and had very little money.

There was a sense of hopelessness in the air, but also a sense that they had nothing to lose. The pupils were open with me; they told me about their lives in their essays, about "mooching" – scouting around town looking for cars to break into – and "skanking" – breaking into shops. They were pathetically grateful for the positive comments I would always put at the end of their work. They liked listening to me read and tell stories from Arthurian legends.


## THE BRIEF RETURN OF JESSE

Jesse's cheeks were caked in make-up. He had really tried his best to look presentable but the overall effect of so much foundation paint and eyeliner was disastrous; he looked a bit like a clown pretending to be a teacher. He was wearing the same oatmeal jacket, the same worn-out corduroys and the same knackered clogs and yet his face was brightly painted.

He hadn't been in school for three weeks. I had taken over his GCSE classes and had managed to read *A Taste Of Honey*, watch the video and start some coursework on the play, and although the class wasn't madly enthusiastic, they weren't openly rebellious. Things were ticking over. I was beginning to develop a quality which has stood me in good stead over the years: the ability to keep ploughing on, to keep turning up, to carry on regardless of what was happening around me, to avoid becoming too worried if I wasn't the most inspired teacher in the world but to just arrive on time, set suitable work and mark it.

Jesse observed me teach the classes that day. He sat in a chair in the corner of the classroom and appeared to nod off every now and then. At the end of the day, he said that he thought I had done well, that he was aware that the classes weren't entirely sure whether to like me or not, but that they respected the fact that I was setting appropriate work. Then he invited me out for a drink with his boyfriend Fred later that evening.

# DID MY BABBLING FINISH OFF JESSE STEVENS?

Fred had a long ponytail like me, but the rest of his head was shaven and his ears dripped with jagged earrings. He was much younger than Jesse and much more aggressive in looks and manner. I wouldn't have guessed he was gay from the way he behaved. After a couple of drinks in a grotty pub in the centre of Coventry, my tongue loosened and I told Jesse about all the rumours that were flying around the school about him. I said that I had heard that he had had a "coming-out" party while he was Head of English at his previous school – a much better school than Oakway Grove – and that the authorities had sacked him because there had been some orgy there. I didn't mention his wife but I was very curious to hear about her; I still wasn't sure whether she was dead or not.

Jesse fluttered his eyelashes over his pint of John Smith's and said, "Tongues do seem to have been wagging, don't they?"

Jesse pretended not to mind me bringing it up, but I know now that hearing this stuff wounded him deeply. Jesse denied that he had been sacked: there had just been a parting of ways and he had got another job. But he was evasive and did admit that there had been a "coming-out" party to which pupils had been invited.

Then we got on to talking about the homophobia that was endemic in schools. The Headmistress at Oakway Grove, who was on secondment while I was there, had ordered Jesse into her office and requested that he stopped wearing his earrings. Jesse had refused and she got defensive, saying, "If you think this is about you being openly homosexual, I can assure you it isn't. Some of my best friends are gay."

At this point, Fred piped up and said, "She needs her lights punched out."

"Oh, don't say that, Fred, she's a friend of my wife's. I don't think you should speak of her like that," Jesse said, soothing his boyfriend by stroking his sleeve. "My wife and she are still good friends."

So the wife was still alive! For some reason, this made me feel very relieved. The rest of the evening was much jollier. We talked about all the poets who were gay and landed up laughing drunkenly about some Latin poet's description of "peachy bottoms".

However, Jesse didn't appear at school the next day. I was informed by the acting Head that he had got a doctor's note that meant he wouldn't be in for the rest of the term. Had my recounting all that school gossip been too much for him?

# GOLDFINGER

Cynthia James held up her index finger to the light. A long, brightly painted gold fingernail glittered underneath the strip-lighting of the classroom. She patted her bouffant hairdo with her other hand as she swept the gold finger down before the mesmerised class.

"Do you see this gold finger here? This is my weapon against all of you who don't learn your vocabulary. You will suffer the goldfinger! Right, I want 32 different words for "said" in the next two minutes. I will go round the class and anyone who doesn't come up with an interesting word for "said" will suffer the gold finger!"

Cynthia's eyes blazed as she waited for the first timorous eleven-year-old to begin. Soon, nearly half the class had come up with lots of words – yell, scream, squeak and so on – and had received copious praise from Cynthia. However, at this point one of the kids froze and couldn't think of a word.

Cynthia stalked over to her in her high heels and leaned down into the poor child's face. "You will suffer the gold finger! My first victim!" Then she scraped her ridiculously long and golden false fingernail against the desk. She did this very lightly so as not to damage the fingernail but the effect was quite unpleasant; the desk emitted a nasty squeaky hiss.

"Do I expect you to talk?" Cynthia mused. "No, I expect you to die!"

None of the petrified children quite got the joke but I found it hilarious.

*\*\**

Cynthia James was aware that she was a con artist, that all her techniques were a kind of bluff. Her teaching was a kind of sorcery; it was all smoke and mirrors which worked with younger kids but was useless with the Daryl Joneses of this world. Cynthia's attitude with them was entirely different; very low-key. She set the work, supervised it and never tried to dominate.

Professor Holmes observed me teach the classes I shared with Cynthia and was most impressed. I explained to Cynthia that Holmes wanted to see my group work – something she never, ever did with the kids – and she laughed. "Group work it will be!" she said, with a magnificent wave of her hand.

She scared the living daylights out of the children

before Holmes's visit. "You will be working in groups and you will co-operate. There will be no squabbles. You will do exactly what Mr Gilbert says. If you don't, I will smile and be nice to you in that lesson. Have no fear about that. But afterwards it will be a different matter. I am a magistrate. I send people to prison in my spare time. I know how to get people. I also have a gold finger!"

She didn't need to do this but her sense of drama always got the better of her. She winked at me at the end of the speech. Goldfinger himself could not have had more obedient servants during the lesson Holmes observed. My group work task, which involved getting the kids to make a radio documentary about an important news story, was perfect.

At the end of the lesson, Holmes looked like he had tears in his eyes. It did take place after lunch and he probably had had a few but I thought he was actually crying when he said, "Francis, I have misjudged you. I thought you were a troublemaker but now I can see I was wrong. You are a good teacher. I know all about what has gone on here and I am proud of the effort you have put in. You have given these children the tools of rationality; the ability to negotiate, the willingness to take responsibility for their actions and you have fostered their creativity. Well done! I think I can safely say that barring any mishaps you have passed the course."

I had another term to complete but it wasn't an arduous affair. I wrote a few essays on my experiences and the lectures I had listened to. I played the game and wrote nothing controversial about child-centred learning and, as a consequence, graduated in August.


## PART TWO

## KNICKER ELASTIC

Joan ushered me into her office. She grabbed me by the arms and told me to stand still. I looked at her in astonishment. Who was this woman? Why was she touching me in such a mumsy fashion?

"So they've picked you, have they?" she said, narrowing her eyes at me. I guessed she was in her mid-forties. She was dressed in a smart, woollen skirt suit and had the bustling manner of a secretary who organised absolutely everything.

"I guess so. Looks like a nice school," I replied. I was feeling pretty good about myself because not only had I just got my haircut – after a four-year hiatus – but the new haircut, a freshly ironed Paisley shirt and jeans and a confident interview had got me my first permanent teaching job.

Joan harrumphed. "So you think that this school looks good, do you? Wait until you start teaching here," she said in a jovial, half-kidding, half-serious way.

"They gave me a tour. All of the kids were working quietly, the classrooms seemed nice. Everyone is friendly. It seems like a great place," I protested.

To be honest, I hadn't expected the Peter Truss Secondary School to appear quite so pleasant. I had applied for a post teaching English and English as a second language at the school because I wanted to continue the work I had done in Coventry saving the country's working classes. I wanted to enjoy that feeling of being really needed that I had found so energising at Coventry. I wanted to surf the crashing waves of poverty and social deprivation and land on the shore laughing.

So it was a bit of a disappointment to find that the Truss School seemed to have been getting along just fine without me, despite the fact that the children in it were among the poorest in Europe. Before my interview I had been shown round the school and had seen studious Bengali children beavering away in more or less total silence.

During the interview, the Headmistress, a huge woman who reminded me of Bagpuss because there was a saggy, genial air about her, had asked me about how I might teach a Bangladeshi child who had just arrived in England the English language. I had responded that I would use flash cards and word games to get them interested.

Now though, Joan, the Headmistress's personal assistant, was telling me that I had gleaned a false idea about the school. "You look young and lively to me. This school will soon see about that," she said and then, while she was digging out my contract from a drawer, she hailed me over and showed me a roll of elastic that was in the drawer. "You know what that is, do you?" I said I didn't.

"It's knicker elastic. I have to keep a roll of it here because the Head is always snapping hers. That's the kind of thing I have to do in this place."

I laughed uneasily. Joan scrutinised me for a while wearing a sheepish and slightly malevolent grin. "Now if you don't run having heard that, you'll be all right," she said. "Congratulations! Welcome to the Cuss School!"

"Cuss? Isn't it Truss?"

"Truss by name, Cuss by nature!" Joan opined.

## NEW LIFE

In September of 1991, my new life as a teacher in inner-city London began. I found a place to stay in a small flat in Kings Cross, which I shared with a friend from university. My basement room was tiny and dark with scarcely enough room for a bed and a desk. The rest of the flat was pretty grotty and fairly dirty.

Every morning I would wake up, grab a bowl of cornflakes and, donning my Paisley shirt, corduroy jeans and desert boots, venture out into the Cross – stepping over drug addicts slouched on the pavement, dodging the traffic and descending down into the Underground where I would board the eastbound Hammersmith and City tube.

Compared with Kings Cross, the environs of the East End were relatively salubrious but no less deprived. I would walk down George Lansbury Lane past a box-like council estate, past Nazi graffiti and derelict houses, along a cobbled lane that always seemed to accommodate the burnt-out shell of a car and then I would skirt the edge of a city farm, where the pigs and sheep would snort and baa at me.

The shadow of an ancient church spire always appeared to lour above the rooftops of the school's buildings as I entered the modern precincts of the school. A great cloud of smoke would greet me when I walked into the staffroom and the sounds of jabbering, angry teachers would spice the stale air.

It was a journey that would come to oppress me towards the end of my stay at Truss, but for the first year or so I liked the urban grittiness of it all. I especially liked the extraordinary environment that I now found myself in. I had never seen a school quite like Truss before. I had never walked down school corridors and seen so many brown and black and yellow faces surging towards me. I had never heard so many foreign languages being spoken before. I had never learnt so much about the disparate parts of the globe: Bangladesh, Pakistan, India, Turkey, Somalia, Afghanistan, Yemen, Mauritius, Sri Lanka. I had had no idea that one classroom could contain so many disparate cultures and outlooks.

Bengali pupils from the Sylheti area of Bangladesh mainly populated the school but there were also representative groups from all over the world. The only pupils who seemed to be missing were the white ones; usually there was only one white kid per class.

## COLIN FORBES

Colin patted the back of my hand and said, "Francis, just don't worry about it, just don't worry about it."

I was just recovering from my first lesson with 9A, the only class that I was actually in charge of but also, according to Colin, one of the worst behaved classes in the school. For most of my timetable I was a support teacher helping students with English as a second language to take part in normal English lessons; the deal was that the actual English teacher stayed up front and I sat at the back and worked with the strugglers.

But for 9A the roles were reversed. Colin, who I normally supported, now supported me. My first lesson was disastrous. To be honest, I can't remember much about it, just a lot of kids shouting at me, giggling, fighting, cussing and lobbing books about the room. Not doing any work basically; they scarcely peeped at the class reader, *Friend or Foe*, which I set before them. Because I had never met the pupils and didn't know who they were, everything felt blurred and out of focus. Over time, my vision of what was really going on would become very sharp, too sharp perhaps. But not in those first weeks.

Colin had sat at the back trying to help two bemused children who spoke no English to read, while I tried unsuccessfully to calm things down.

I was distraught by the end of the lesson but Colin made a special point of comforting me. He patted my hand again. I felt very grateful. Even though I had only been at the school a few days, I knew that he was a very busy teacher and highly respected by the rest of the staff; his words of succour counted for a lot.

"It's not your fault, Francis. You were told by your head of department to read this book to them and really they weren't the slightest bit interested in it. Why should a group of Bengali teenagers be remotely attracted by a novel about evacuees during wartime? You need to go back to your head of department and ask him for a decent scheme of work that actually might interest this lot," he said.

I nodded. I actually wasn't quite sure whether Colin was right about *Friend or Foe*, which seemed to have some parallels with some of these kids' lives, in that it was about children being uprooted from their cultures and flung into an alien situation, but I didn't mention this. Yes, Colin was right. I needed to tackle my elusive head of department about finding some decent materials for these kids.

Colin leaned back in his alloted chair in the staff-room and sucked in the nicotine-perfumed air that always lingered in the smokers' corner. Although Colin was not a smoker, he preferred to sit amidst clouds of cigarette smoke because all his friends enjoyed a puff or two. He patted the patterned jumper that covered his ample belly. He was a chunky avuncular man in his early forties who was going bald and had a face that looked like a boxer's. His buckled nose and tough-guy eyes reminded me a lot of Bob Hoskins.

"That's what you've got to do my boy. Go and see your head of department," he said, chortling with a high degree of conspiratorial bonhomie. At that point some of his friends trooped in, fags already hanging from the corners of their mouths. They lit up as Colin merrily recounted what had happened to me.

"Poor old Francis here has suffered at the hands of 9A and you know who I blame. It's your head of department, Joe Dicey. He should have devised some decent schemes of work to keep a class like that happy," Colin said.

"Poor Francis," exclaimed Pam Drabble, a drama teacher who I supported in a few drama lessons. She sat down beside Colin, blew out some smoke, and patted his knee in a friendly fashion and said, "Yes, you're quite right. Joe really needs to give his teachers some decent material to teach."

"But the question is, will he ever do that?" Colin said, wrinkling his forehead. "Maybe Francis will be the impetus for him to sort things out... Go on, boy, do your thing! Go and mount an attack on the man in the stock cupboard!"

Perhaps now, with the benefit of hindsight, I can see just how Colin manipulated me, but then I had no idea what was going on. Staffroom hierarchies are very powerful and largely unspoken things; the only thing I was aware of back then was that Colin was near the top of the hierarchy and someone I needed to obey if I was going to keep in with the "decent" teachers.

The rest of the smokers roared with laughter; they were used to Colin behaving like this and seemed to revel in his antics. I felt uneasy but attempted to join in the fun by carrying out Colin's instructions.

# A TRIP TO THE STOCK CUPBOARD

I left the staffroom and entered the main corridor of the school. I still felt rather bewildered by everything. The smell of curry and cheap school uniforms and old battered trainers swept through the air, together with a jumbled, jumpy morass of skinny pupils who were chattering away in numerous tongues: Bengali, Somali, Turkish and Cockney. They pushed past me as I hesitated about what to do.

Should I go and see Joe Dicey? I had already heard that he was a very odd chap who had hidden himself away in the English stock cupboard for the past thirty years. I gasped. He had already been Head of English for eight years when I was born. I met the Headmistress shuffling along the corridor at the bottom of the stairs. I said hello and told her that I was looking for Joe Dicey and asked her where his stock cupboard was. The Headmistress harrumphed. She was out of breath and obviously wasn't enjoying the sensation of having so many kids pushing past her. But she did agree to show me the hallowed venue.

She headed for the lift that was situated just opposite the stairs. I followed her but she stopped me with a slow wave of her hand at the threshold of the lift.

"Sorry, the lift is only for senior staff," she said. "I'll see you on the first floor." I apologised. She seemed rather aggrieved that I hadn't known such a piece of information. But it certainly wasn't in the staff handbook.

Having fought past the squabbling kids on the stairs, I met her on the first floor and she directed me to Dicey's cupboard before disappearing into another cupboard.[1]


## INTO THE DARKNESS

I coughed. In the dim light, I could see that the stock cupboard was much larger than I had supposed. Metal racks which housed tatty piles of ancient textbooks stretched back far into the room. Behind a couple of racks, I could see that a bare light bulb was shining on a mop of pure white hair. A tall figure was

---

1.The mystical truths about school cupboards: The school cupboard is a very peculiar thing. The mind boggles at all that goes on in school cupboards during any given day. They are the only truly private places in schools except for toilet cubicles and because of this, they are the venues for the most interesting activities: one-to-one tuition, whispering gossips, illicit drug-taking, desperate embraces and rapidly snatched copulations, quiet sobs and hard-won bars of chocolate.

sitting hunched at a desk gazing at the *Daily Express*. It was Joe Dicey.

Dicey was a handsome man who looked rather like Gandalf: he had a wizard's prominent nose and wise eyes and grizzled demeanour. He was also surprisingly stylish and casual in his dress; he wore ironed black jeans, a tasteful black jumper and open-neck shirt that revealed a muscular chest. He had quite a commanding physical presence. He put down the paper as I approached.

"Ah yes, do come in, do come in," he murmured in a friendly voice, waving his arm.

"I just wanted to talk to you about 9A. I just had a tricky lesson with them. Colin said that you might have some material that might interest them a little more than the book I am reading," I said.

Dicey blinked. Suddenly his face looked inexpressibly weary. He didn't want to be dealing with this. He asked what book I was reading with them and I told him.

"Now, *Friend or Foe* is not a bad little book. Let me see now," he said and reached for his register. "Yes, I read *Joby*, *The Wizard of Earthsea*, *Buddy*, *Macbeth* and *Oliver Twist* with them last year."

I was staggered. "How on earth did you do that?"

"It's very simple really. You just hand out the book and read to them. They like it. If they don't, just shout at them or phone their parents. I never had a problem."

Dicey's tone wasn't sarcastic but nor was it helpful. He was simply stating how things were for him. I already knew that there must be something amiss with what he was saying because it was clear to me that at least ten pupils could not read or write, let alone tackle Dickens and Shakespeare.

"But what about the ESL (English as Second Language) kids?"

Dicey picked up his paper again and began to read, "I'd go and see the Head of ESL about them. Or Colin. Isn't he supporting you in that class? Colin knows what's what."

As far as Dicey was concerned the conversation was over. The *Express* rose over his face. I retreated away from the bare light bulb and back out into the corridor.


## PERKY PERCY

I had already gleaned from the smokers' corner that the Head of ESL was nicknamed Perky Percy and once I met him on his "home turf" – in the ESL room –

I could see why he enjoyed this sobriquet. Mr Jonty Percy was the total opposite to Joe Dicey. Whereas Dicey liked nothing better than to hide away in his stock cupboard, Percy loved wandering around his ESL 'resources' room, chatting to his staff (who were numerous, the ESL department being the biggest in the school) and assisting the forlorn kids who came in for help with homework. His room was awash with the latest textbooks and displays, the most recent government documents and banners that celebrated the languages spoken in the school.

He dusted the chalk off his powder-blue suit and listened to me intently as I explained my problem.

"What we need here is some differentiation! Differentiation!" he proclaimed brightly. "And, as luck would have it, I have just received the latest government directive on such matters. I invite you to peruse it at your leisure, my dear sir!"

I didn't know what differentiation meant so I took the document and started to read it immediately. The words in the booklet swam before my eyes; I found it impossible to decipher any of it, apart from the fact that differentiation apparently meant that the teacher had to adapt existing books into simple language and pictures so that ESL students could understand them. I looked up from the desk. It was nearly the end of lunch. Outside rain clouds were gathering above the grim spire of St Anthony's Church, lots of kids were squabbling and giggling in the grey, high-fenced yard of the playground and in the far distance the light on the top of the Canary Wharf tower was blinking on and off.

I caught up with Percy just as he was departing to register his tutor group.

"So what this book is basically saying is that I should rewrite *Friend or Foe* in simple language for the language learners or draw pictures to help them understand it?"

"Yes, differentiate, differentiate. That's the name of the game these days!"

"But that's a massive task…" I said.

"Colin will help you. He's a good man, Colin," Percy said, and disappeared from view before I could ask any more.


## BACK TO COLIN

It wasn't until early the next morning that I caught up with Colin. He lived in Norfolk and had to set off from his house in the country at four in the morning in order to beat the traffic. As a consequence he generally arrived at the school at about half-past six. Realising that most of the teachers I dealt with arrived early and departed early, I adjusted my alarm clock and started to arrive at the school at about seven-thirty. Past the druggies in King's Cross and into the vandalised dereliction of the East End.

Colin was sitting in his big, ancient armchair cradling a cup of foaming instant soup. His eyes were bright with laughter. He was chatting to Pam Drabble and Phillis Gooch, the portly Head of Home Economics. I couldn't be sure what they were laughing about but I hoped it wasn't me. I ventured to sit beside him and told him that I had been instructed to differentiate. Colin stopped laughing and said, "Of course, that's the whole point."

"So that's what's we're going to do, then?" I asked.

For some reason, I felt reluctant about asking Colin explicitly to help adapt the book. I couldn't be sure what his reaction would be."Yes. Of course," Colin said and then, turning to Phillis, remarked, "Well, my girlfriend wasn't too happy when I told her where to get off. I just said, 'I'm finished with you.'"

More laughter from the cackling smokers. It was

clear that Colin felt that my conversation with him was finished. I got up to go. Just as I was leaving the smokers' corner, Colin acknowledged my departure by saying, "Don't worry, Francis, I'll take care of things with 9A."

## CONFUSED

I sat back on my seat in the non-smoking part of the staffroom. I was confused and anxious. I had 9A again that morning and was none the wiser about how to teach them. I felt that I had only myself to blame. I should know how to differentiate, I should know how to read Shakespeare to them without enduring a murmur, I should know how to get them to behave...

I looked at the vision before me; the staffroom table was heaped with scrappy files, torn textbooks, mouldy cups of coffee, and a couple of sports' holdalls from which some smelly trainers were protruding. Outside, it was beginning to rain. From this vantage point I could see the city farm that was opposite the school. A couple of pigs were snorting about in a great trough of mud. They were dirty and looked unhappy and imprisoned.

Just like me. But a rising sense of panic about facing the class curtailed my seizure of self-pity. I gripped the miserable novel, *Friend or Foe*, grabbed a piece of paper and scanned the chapter we were to read next lesson. Having perused it, I wrote a summary of it, leaving blanks at important places, and wrote out the words that needed to go in the blanks at the bottom of the page together with a series of ridiculous stick-men illustrations that showed the action of the chapter in a moderately visual fashion. Having finished this, I rushed to the photocopier and copied thirty sheets ready for my class.

## YER MUM

"Yer mum is a cock-sucking whore who sucks cocks."

"Yer mum is a cock-sucking whore who takes it up the bum."

"Yer mum is a cock-sucking bum bandit whore who takes it up the bum and more."

"Yer mum is a cocksucker."

"Yer mum sucks cocks."

"Yer mum is a whore."

"Yer mum!"

"Yer mum!"

"YER MUM!"

"YER MUM!"

"Sir, sir, Bulus just cussed my mum."

"He started it!"

"He said, 'yer mum' to me!"

"He said it too!"

I had been hearing this developing conversation, but pretended not to hear it because I was busy trying to explain to Ikram that my two stick men were the two boys in the story *Friend or Foe* and the big stick man was the farmer who took them to live on his farm. Ikram was shaking his head in disbelief and laughing at the sheer incompetence of my drawing. At this point, Colin had lumbered over. Ikram was one of his brood – an ESL learner who really only knew three words of English: "fuck" and "yer mum". Colin sat beside Ikram and laughed along.

"Shall we see if we can do a better drawing?" Colin suggested. Ikram nodded his head and together they set about drawing the two boys.

My worksheet seemed to have done the trick – at least partially. 9A was very noisy but nearly everyone was attempting to write the fill-in-the-gaps exercise into their books. However, there was this situation with Bulus and Mohibur's mothers to sort out.

Bulus was a fat boy with lots of black bum fluff swimming around his face; he had a comic appearance and reminded me of an adolescent Bengali version of Oliver Hardy. Evidently Mohibur thought something similar because it was already clear to me that he was always making fun of him. Judging from Bulus's apoplectic face and Mohibur's cool grin, I could see who was winding up whom.

"He said 'yer mum' to me," Bulus repeated defensively.

Mohibur claimed that Bulus had started it. I had already realised that this imprecation was by far the worst that could be hurled at someone around here; saying that someone's mother was sexually active and possibly adulterous, or made money by selling her body, was tantamount to saying that their offspring was a worthless joke. In this culture – not just the Bengali culture but East End culture – mothers were sacrosanct; they were the people who held everything together, who reared children, who fed them, who made money for them. They had the status of sacred beings once a child entered the circumference of the school; they were magically transfigured into paragons of virtue and saintliness. Therefore anyone who criticised them, or more especially suggested that they were not pure and free from sexual desires, was committing a blasphemy.

Such blasphemies were very common at Peter "Cuss". I decided that I would try and stop these ones by moving Mohibur to another part of the classroom. He protested that he hadn't actually done anything wrong and refused to move. I tried to ask Bulus to move but he refused by shaking his head and folding his arms. It was an exasperating situation. I went over to Colin and told him what had happened. Colin nodded knowingly and went to speak to the boys. I got on with helping the others while he talked to them.

At the end of the lesson, I noticed that they hadn't moved and asked Colin what he had said to them. He smiled. "I sorted it out. It's all right now," he said.

For some reason, I didn't want to know how he had done this, I just trusted that he had.


THINGS BEGIN TO WORK

Because they were the only class that I actually "properly" taught, 9A came to dominate my thoughts. I read up about how to differentiate materials for ESL learners and spent many hours every week writing out worksheets that would assist them with understanding *Friend or Foe*. I tried to vary the activities by asking them to do different exercises every lesson: putting parts of the story in the right order, comprehension questions, writing diaries of the characters' thoughts and feelings and so on.

I also started to use these techniques for the classes that I supported, producing worksheets for my pupils to complete as they worked through the reading of a text. There was never much marking to do because the students produced so little writing, and what little writing they did do could easily be marked in the class with the pupil listening to my comments.

And, by and by, all the effort I put in with the worksheets began to pay off. As Colin noted, my pupils were actually learning to write and this gave them a sense of satisfaction which pushed them into writing more. I realised that Joe Dicey had done nothing but read his favourite texts with the class and had never invited them to do any writing except for copying from the board.

But I could never say that it was easy.

# A TYPICALLY STRESSFUL AFTERNOON

Let me describe a particular afternoon that is typical of the more troubled ones in a young teacher's life. I've been teaching 9A for a few months now. We are nearly at the end of *Friend or Foe*. My mental telescope is starting to focus properly upon the class, the blurred threatening shapes have become real people who are increasingly sharply defined.

My heart starts racing as I leave the staffroom and mount the stairs. Lunch is over. There is no escape. The sounds and smells of the school whoosh past me in an ectoplasmic haze; uniforms graze against my arms, the strip lights of the corridor dazzle my eyes, the smell of boiled sweets and spices and the fugginess of rooms with steamed windows pass through me.

There they are jostling against the corridor wall, prodding each other, guffawing and shuffling about as they wait to be let into the room. There are twenty-four brown faces, who are mostly boys, and two white ones – two white girls. One of the girls, Charlene Smith, a pinched-faced skinny girl with a scab on her chin and a filthy blouse, winks at me: "Anyone tell you, you got a nice arse sir?" She winks at me again.

I don't smile. Oh shit, I think, the lesson hasn't

started and I need to sort her out. What should I do with her? Send her to her "housemaster", Phil Strong, the person who was supposed to deal with disciplinary problems? I scan the corridor and see that Colin is nowhere around. He's always late. I notice that no one has actually heard her say this except her friend, Leticia Green, who is leering at me in a similar way. Leticia never says anything in lessons and never does anything either – all of which makes me inclined to leave her alone.

I try to make out that I haven't heard Charlene's comment and let the class into the room. As they pass into the scruffy classroom, Wahid notes, "You got red eyes sir! Very red eyes! Anything the matter with you? You sick? You got someone sick about you sir? You not infected are you?"

Wahid gestures wildly with his arms and his friends start to join in by pointing at their eyes and saying, "Red eyes! Red eyes!"

This is something they say a lot because my red eyes are quite noticeable. For some reason, since I have started at Truss, I have suffered from red eyes. This isn't because I am drinking heavily and nor is it conjunctivitis; it is a Truss-related condition that neither I nor my doctor can get to the bottom of.

Once they are all safely ensconced in the classroom, I hand out the textbooks and their classbooks – neither of which I allow home because they always disappear. Homework does not happen in this school except in policy documents. At this point, Colin surfaces, smiling and chuckling and patting his big belly contentedly. He takes a seat next to Ikram as I begin: "Now 9A, I need you to listen. Could you listen please? Sharif, please could you stop hitting Bilal with your book. Your book is for reading. Turn to page forty-five please. Now, Wahid, where had we got to in the story? What was happening?"

As well as being the one who notices my red eyes, Wahid is also one of the few pupils who remembers what is going on in the book.

"It is about these boys and they don't know whether the enemy is really their enemy. He might be their friend. And their friends might be their enemies."

"Very good, Wahid. Sharif, I hope you were listening to that! Jafar, don't flick! I said no elastic bands! And stop tapping Fotik! Stop it! Now!"

Wahid and his friends start laughing at my sudden explosion. I walk over to Fotik who is threatening to flick an elastic band at Bulus. I point to the page in the book we are about to read. I ask little Sharif, a cheeky tiny kid with a cherubic face and a habit of being naughty if he isn't kept occupied, to read. The lesson continues. The class settles down to listening to the story and would continue to listen if we weren't interrupted by a blonde woman in black jeans and silver earrings entering the room.

"Oh fucking hell," Charlene mutters under her breath. It's Charlene's Educational Welfare Officer, her EWO. For reasons that no one has told me, Charlene has an EWO who tracks her in lessons. From what I can see the woman does more harm than good, because Charlene always becomes even more agitated when she is in the room. But she is quite an attractive lady with sexy blue eyes and a Marilyn Monroe smile and, such is the dearth of fanciable ladies in Truss, I find myself smiling gingerly back at her and running to her defence when Charlene becomes bolshy.

Charlene snarls when I tell her to get on with the work, that it's boring and she isn't going to do anything. She then turns to the EWO and says conspiratorially, "Don't you think that sir has a nice arse?"

The EWO snorts and breaks into an hysterical giggle. She reddens and then tells Charlene to start reading the book. "You do, doncha? You do, doncha?" Charlene says, grinning broadly and revealing her broken front teeth. I move away quickly, not wanting to be drawn further into the worrying world of Charlene Smith's burgeoning sexual predilections.

There is another tussle developing between Bulus and Mohibur. Bulus has developed the idea that maybe it might be fun to rip the cover off his *Friend or Foe*, roll it into a cone and whack Mohibur on the head with it.

"You're going to have to pay for that book," I say to Bulus, realising the moment I have said this that I won't be able to carry out this threat. Bulus's parents barely have enough money to pay for clean socks for him, let alone fork out for books.

Bulus shrugs and continues hitting Mohibur. "Can you stop that, please?" I say in quite a conciliatory way. Just at that moment I catch Colin's gaze; he is looking at the door.

Oh my God! It is my probationary adviser, Tom Hardy, who has just walked in. I had no idea that he was due to observe me today

Oh fuck. This is the man who will pass or fail my probationary year; he is a local authority inspector and English adviser who has to write a report on me upon which my whole career in teaching hinges. He is a bald, softly spoken man who wears Hush Puppies and has a cadaverous, sallow face and small, black eyes which are now staring at me, analysing me, dismantling me bit by bit.

I had been dealing with Bulus's assault on Mohibur in a relatively relaxed fashion but now I feel I am being scrutinised, I go into overdrive. "Bulus! Just stop that now! We have work to do!" I shout at the top of my voice.

Everyone in the class suddenly takes notice and stares at Bulus's table where I am standing. "Right 9A, it's time to write a newspaper article about the discovery of the Germans' airplane which has crashed in the woods."

As usual I have a specially made-up worksheet that basically does most of the work but leaves out some blanks at some key places. My idea is that the ESL kids will have the worksheet and the more able will try and write a newspaper article by themselves. But this doesn't work out as planned because Wahid leads the charge for the worksheet.

"Wahid, you're not to have the worksheet! You have to do it by yourself!"

"But I don't understand. I need the worksheet. I'm lonely without it!" he says with mock mournfulness. I don't want another altercation so I give him the worksheet and then realise that I'll have to give everyone one. I had foreseen this eventuality and had photocopied enough for the whole class.

Wahid, Sharif, Bilal and Yumni finish filling in the blanks in five minutes and rather than going onto the extension exercise that I have set them – which is, surprise, surprise, to write their own newspaper article – they start making paper aeroplanes with the work-sheets. I end up shouting at them to stop it; this is partially successful and they begin, albeit in the most reluctant fashion, to scrawl their own newspaper articles into their books.

When the bell goes at the end of the lesson, the pupils suddenly disappear like bathwater down the plughole before I can set imaginary homework. Colin plods after them with a knowing grin, followed by the EWO who asks me in a hapless voice whether I know where Charlene Smith went, and then Tom Hardy.

Tom Hardy lingers. "I'm sorry I was late," he says, "But I had to speak to your head teacher. Have you got a moment now?"

I haven't, technically; I'm supposed to be supporting Eddie Figgis with his GCSE class. But I am anxious to know what Hardy has to say, so I mumble that perhaps I could listen to him for a few minutes.

"The thing is, Francis, I think there are some issues here. I don't think that you're handling this class very well."

He pauses to let these words sink in. His comment is irritating and unfair and something I could very well do without.

But I have learnt from Holmes the dangers in pissing off advisers, so I keep quiet.

"Yes," I say, weakly.

"You shouldn't be shouting at these children in the way you are. It is highly confrontational and not productive. I have great reservations about the way you differentiate. You gave out those worksheets to pupils who should have written their own newspaper articles. You didn't challenge those pupils and that led to classroom management issues. Your classroom management and differentiation need addressing."

My blood tries to punch holes in the walls of my veins. I feel like head-butting this twerp. But I do nothing. I nod grimly, repeating his miserable education-speak: "Differentiation and classroom management." Basically, he means that the content of my lesson was shit and the kids were fucking around like crazy.

Hardy gazes pensively at the window as if immersed

in the brilliancy of his observations. Outside, in the gathering November dusk, a police helicopter is buzzing around over the ramshackled rooftops of the East End. Standing in the empty classroom, I marvel at the serenity of Hardy and of the sudden peace. Just a moment ago, the world was in a state of uproar; now it is silent. All around the walls and ceiling of the room seem to be growling in a muffled fashion as the noise of the school impacts upon them.

"I've got to go now. I've got a lesson to teach," I say, swallowing a lump in my throat. I feel sorry for myself; the bastard could have at least said one positive thing.

Hardy turns away from the window and dips into his briefcase. "I think you need to read this. You need to do more group work with these children. Their learning is far too passive at the moment," he says, and hands me a sheaf of photocopies.

"Thanks," I say. "Thanks very much."

For the first time, he smiles, albeit in a world-weary way. Suddenly I realise something about him. He needs to criticise me in order to feel like he is doing a good job and he needs me to be grateful.

I slip out of the room and run along the corridor to my next lesson.

Just as I am about to enter the room, I find a skinny Bengali kid, Hakim, and his bobble hat hurtling at me, followed by the bellowing form of an irate teacher wearing a Clash T-Shirt and a silver jacket. Hakim is a rough, tough kid who isn't the slightest bit scared. But Edward Figgis, while he may not frighten his pupils, gives me the heebie-jeebies. I find it so difficult to reconcile his appearance – the punky T-shirts, the flash jackets, the DMs, the earrings – and his manner. He is an abrasive character who exudes hair-trigger aggression; as his support teacher, I can never be sure whether he'll lose his temper with me or not. I have seen him explode at a couple of other teachers for comparatively trivial reasons and I definitely don't want to be on the wrong end of his wrath.

I apologise for being late before he can have a go at me for that. But he is too immersed in assailing Hakim to notice me inching into the classroom. Inside, I find the class listening silently to the fireworks outside. I ask Jamal what had happened.

"Hakim said bogga at Figgis," Jamal said with a grin.

*Bogga* is one of the only words in Bengali that I

know; it means "penis". I have to work hard to stop myself from grinning too. I scan all the eyes in the classroom and see that many of the kids are watching me, checking out my reaction. I shudder. Suddenly, I realise that I have misjudged them; they feel exactly the same way about Figgis as I do. I realise that for all our differences in age, social class, upbringing, status and wealth, we are all fundamentally the same in our emotions: Figgis freaks us out. We share a common humanity. We don't like the way Figgis is bawling out Hakim, even if he deserves it.

The helicopter is back again. Just as Figgis re-enters the room, all of the kids rush up to the window and point to the thudding, rotating blades. I watch Figgis look at them and think about shouting at them to go and sit in their seats, but then I see that he doesn't have the energy. He doesn't acknowledge me but goes to his desk and sits down on his chair, pulls out a sheaf of papers from his desk and starts perusing them.

Realising that he needs a break, I walk up to the pupils and ask them to sit down in a soft, conciliatory voice. But I am drawn to the helicopter. It is, after all, quite a fantastic sight. The last dregs of the winter sunlight are splashing over the frosty, dilapidated roofs and there is a spotlight shining out of the belly of the 'copter. What the hell is going on over there?

"They're coming for you Hakim," Figgis says, peering up from his papers. A victorious grin spreads across his face. His earring glints. He bashes his fist into his palm and adds: "No, in fact, they're coming for... yer mum!"

Hakim stands sheepishly in the corner of the room, trying to shake off the insult with a sarcastic smirk, "Oh very funny, Figgis! Yer so funny!"

But Hakim finds to his surprise that the class isn't on his side with this one. Now that the helicopter has disappeared, Figgis's joke has drawn their attention. They point and jeer at Hakim as they return to their seats. Hakim quivers. Suddenly I feel sorry for him. A moment ago, notwithstanding the provocation of his teacher, he seemed like a nasty, cynical yob but now he is a frightened gangly boy who is wearing cheap trainers, no socks, ripped trousers and a dirty shirt. He shuffles to his seat and sits down.

Somehow, amidst all this uproar, the kids manage to return to their work. They continue writing their autobiographies. I sit with my group of ESL kids and help them transcribe theirs.

# AUTOBIOGRAPHIES

When I look back on it, one of the most extraordinary things about being an ESL teacher was the amount of individual attention I could give the kids.

Sitting with my group – Faisel, Fotik, Abbas and Jafar – at the back of Figgis's classroom, I was able to piece together these boys' lives for them. I would question them.

"Where were you born?"

"In Sylhet," Fotik said.

"In Somalia," Abbas said.

"In Birmingham," Faisel said.

And Jafar would always shake his head. He spoke virtually no English. No one knew what age he was. He was a tiny, baby-faced boy who was swamped by his uniform; his hands did not reach out of his sleeves and he regularly tripped over his trousers.

***

I asked the boys about their earliest memories and quite quickly, through detailed questioning, frag-mented, intense pictures of their lives arose before our eyes out of the graffitied formica desks and incessant chitter-chatter and clatter of the class. My pupils provided the information and I transcribed.

Fotik: I remember Grandpa picking snakes out of a bucket. He smelt of wet, muddy fields and always carried around a long gnarled stick, which he called his wand. He would poke and investigate the snakes with the stick, talking to them, soothing them, laughing with them. I would go with him to market to sell the snakes. The women always said he sold the freshest snakes in Sylhet. They would ask him to kill them before their very own eyes so that they could be sure the snake was fresh, then they would take them home and make snake curry with them. Snake makes a good fishy-tasting curry. I would recommend it. But you don't have it here in England; you will have to go to Bangladesh for that.

Abbas: There was burning. The smell of burning. I was screaming. I can remember feeling the scorching of the fire; it felt like it was eating up my arm like some hungry monster. The house was on fire. Some soldiers had decided that it might be fun to set our house alight. I watched them laughing as the dry wattle roof and floor of our bedroom burned. My mother didn't cry but seeing that I was hurting she picked me up and jumped out of the window. The soldiers carried on laughing but they didn't shoot at us with their rifles. My father had gone. I don't know what happened to him. After that we didn't go back to the house but kept moving, always moving on.

It took a lot of effort to get this information out of them – they didn't volunteer it freely. They had no conception that what had happened to them might be of interest to a wider audience, but were clearly impressed when I typed up their stories and put them in their coursework folders. A year later, when the school was inspected, the inspectors commended these autobiographies. Well, maybe I had ghostwritten them – but I felt as if they were genuine pieces of work.

## SURFACING

At the time, I didn't appreciate just how effective Figgis's apparently haphazard methods were. I didn't see how his more informal teaching style meant that I had more freedom to really engage with the kids. I remember the noise and chaos ringing in my ears as I tried to delve into these kids' remarkable lives. Like a scuba-diver plunging into murky waters, I was able to drop myself down beneath the surface storm and find translucent depths underneath, to shine a torch upon forgotten and neglected parts of these pupils' histories. I had the right equipment: an ability to ignore the noise, a desire to hear what they had to say, a knack of asking the right questions.

Then at the end of the lesson, I would surface, my head heavy and ringing with the effort of it all. Most of the pupils would be gone but Figgis would be there, smiling and slapping his fist into the palm of his hand. He liked to hear about what I had done with the kids.

Today, having been mauled by the softly spoken Tom Hardy and witnessed Figgis's treatment of Hakim, I find his questioning excessively irritating, almost gloating.

"What's it to you?" I say, waiting for the last kids to leave as I collect all the autobiographies together.

Figgis's grin wanes. He slaps his fist more firmly into his palm.

"Are you all right, Francis? Is anything the matter?"

Although he asks this question inviting me to tell the truth, it is clear from his body language, his tight mouth and narrowed eyes, that he doesn't want to hear my answer. I turn away from him and try to joke, "You're too busy messing around with the papers on your desk to see if anything is the matter."

Figgis doesn't reply. My heart thuds as I scan the dark horizon outside for the helicopter. I need to get out of the room as quickly as possible; Figgis is about to go nuclear and I don't want to be irradiated. I edge towards the door and see that Figgis is munching on his lips with his incisors.

"You have no idea what I have been doing. The Head does, though," he hisses. As he says these words, his lips spring out of the vice-like grip of his teeth and shine in the pasty electric light. He looks very tired and very annoyed.

I slip out of the room before the conversation can continue. But as I grab my bag in the staffroom, I regret not asking him what he has been up to. He shields the papers as soon as anyone approaches. He appears to be scribbling away at something. What has all his writing got to do with the Head? It is a complete mystery.


## CONTROL

You only become obsessed with control when you lose it. Until things went seriously wrong – as they were about to – I wasn't too bothered about my ability to "control" a class. After it, my desire for control became an obsession that was to dominate my teaching career for the next few years.

The day after my near run-in with Figgis, he phoned in sick. On reflection, I realised that he hadn't seemed that well in the lesson – more chronically depressed than anything – and I regretted being so tetchy with him. I landed up taking the Year 11 class as the "proper" teacher. Strictly speaking, this wasn't supposed to happen because I was paid to be a support teacher and not a mainstream one, but the school couldn't afford enough supply teachers; it was a bad time of year, November, and a lot of staff were off sick with flu.

Figgis hadn't set any cover work. I was aware that nearly everyone had finished writing their auto-biographies and that part of their rowdiness was due to the fact that they didn't have enough to do. So I decided that they could start reading Arthur Miller's *A View From The Bridge* in groups; this was the play that they needed to study for coursework.

I sat down with my little group of language learners, read some of the play and tried to explain to Jafar that Eddie Carbone was attracted in a physical way to his niece Catherine. This proved difficult and I had to make little suggestive gestures with my eyes and say, "Eddie like Catherine, you know?"

Jafar's eyes lit up and he nodded, saying, "Eddie he wanna fuck Catherine. He wanna fuck. He wanna fuck!"

Hearing Jafar talk like this was shocking not because bad language was rare in the school – it certainly wasn't – but because Jafar was normally so quiet and meek. He shook with the force of this revelation in his oversized school uniform; he pumped his arms, making his hands appear and disappear from the sleeves of his jacket. It was like watching someone have an epileptic fit.

"Jafar, you shouldn't speak like that," I said. "I'll have to send you 'On Call'[2]."

---

2.<u>On Call</u>:This is a system that a lot of schools have but tend to keep quiet about. The idea is that if a pupil gets too rowdy or badly behaved, the teacher should have a place where they can send the pupil.

Usually the "On Call" system is staffed by the senior management of the school, Deputy Heads and Heads of Department and so forth. A timetable of who is "On Call" is written out and given to every teacher, the teacher then knows where and to whom to send the kid at any given lesson. After encountering some loathsome behaviour, the teacher fills in a form writing down the pupil's name, describes the nature of the incident and details what work the kid should get on with. The form is given to the pupil and they go off to "On Call".

That's the theory but, in practice, things are usually more complicated than that. Sometimes the pupil refuses to go and there's a raging argument about whether the kid deserves to go "On Call" or not. Sometimes the teacher doesn't have a timetable of who and where to send the kid to and the kid comes ambling back after a few minutes saying that he can't find "On Call". More trauma then ensues because the teacher has to decide whether he should let the brat back into the room or root around in their chaotic register for the correct piece of paper that tells him the necessary information.

Sometimes the kid gets sent back by the teacher "On Call" because they don't have: a) an "On Call" slip; b) a slip which has been filled in correctly; c) a good enough reason for being sent "On Call"; d) any work to get on with.

It's a real hassle for the teacher "On Call" because he or she has to log the incident in a book and then keep the miscreant quiet.

In Oakway Grove and at another school I taught at, Wickstead, the system worked quite well because there was only one place to send the offender to. Oakway Grove called this place "The Unit"; this was a windowless cell where the child had to sit in silence. In Wickstead, it was the dining hall. The kids and the teachers knew where to go and usually who would be greeting them there; the same people got sent out of lessons time after time and so would usually get a pretty good idea as to who would be there to greet them.

In Truss, the system was a complete shambles because the venue for "On Call" kept changing and often the senior staff wouldn't be in attendance. This meant that for much of the day many of the worst behaved children would be roaming around the school with scraps of pink paper in their hands nominally looking for the teacher "On Call". In reality, they were doing no such thing because they knew that nobody knew who was "On Call" or where it was. Sometimes they would drop into other lessons and give a helping hand to whoever was misbehaving there or they would slink off to the toilets to sniff some glue or have a smoke.

Jafar thought that my threat was not only totally feeble but also quite funny. In fact, as I repeated that I would send him "On Call" this seemed to encourage him even more and caused the rest of the class to scrutinise my merry group of strugglers. It was quite degrading having to threaten Jafar with "On Call" because he wasn't your average "On Call" character; he probably didn't even understand quite what it was.

Now the rest of the class was getting interested. At the beginning of the lesson I had a sense of them being like a choppy, winter sea rolling onto the shore, but now I could feel the wind rising, the water beginning to swirl and waves starting to crash onto the beach and edge towards the town. I felt as if I only had the flimsiest wall to stop the tide from flooding the streets.

I shouted, "Right, quiet now, let's get on with the work!"

There were titters and guffaws. Hakim snorted and then produced a packet of cigarettes.

"If you light that I'll have to send you 'On Call'," I said. My face was red. There was a sense of despair eddying around my stomach. Panic shot through every limb of my body.

Hakim lit the cigarette. It felt as if the dam had burst and cold, stinging water was sloshing around my neck. The whole class stood up and started running around the room, including even Jafar, who was by now shouting at the top of his voice, "Eddie he wanna fuck Catherine! Eddie he wanna fuck Catherine!"

I hated Jafar more than anyone else in the world at that moment. This was the ungrateful runt who I had worked so hard with, who I had so painstakingly tried to educate, who I had written so many fill-in-the-gaps worksheets for; he owed me big-time and how was he repaying me?

The rest of the class began to move the furniture out of the room. I shouted at the top of my voice for them to stop, but it was useless. The desks, the chairs, the board rubber, the textbooks and English folders sailed out of the room on the inexorable tide and ricocheted into the corridor. Only Hakim and his mates remained in the classroom puffing away on their cigarettes.

"Wanna a drag?" Hakim grinned at me.


## REVENGE

Rarely have I felt so bad before or since. As well as feeling totally humiliated, I felt angry and guilty. The guilt was the worst emotion to endure because

I felt as though the whole incident was my fault. Here was I who had been so smugly (but privately) condemning Figgis's lessons for being a shambles and yet, when it came down to it, not only was I worse at control than Figgis, I was probably the worst in the school. I was so ashamed of what had happened that I didn't want to tell anyone about it, I just wanted to slink off home and cry into my pillow for a very long time and never wake up and never teach again.

Fortunately, I wasn't able to do this. Word had got round about the chaos caused in the corridor and I was paid a visit by one of the Deputy Heads, a tough bruiser called John Priest.

Priest was typical of the kind of teacher who ran the schools in the East End of London; a working-class guy with a teaching certificate who, while not massively clever, definitely knew how to deal with difficult kids. He probably had been one himself.

He got some kids to push the furniture back into the room, patted me on the back and said, "Don't worry about it. We'll get them."

The next morning he came in at the beginning of the lesson. Figgis was still off, but this time I had a supply teacher in with me.

There was absolute silence as Priest strode in. He

was a big man who had a definitive air of Michael Caine in *Get Carter* about him.

"You are scum and I don't like scum," he said, continuing, "You behaved like scum yesterday and I am sickened by it. Don't you ever, ever do it again. Is that understood?"

Row after row of delinquent faces nodded meekly.

"Now, who was smoking in the lesson?" Priest asked.

No reply. He knew full well who was smoking but he was doing this for dramatic effect.

"Who was smoking?"

Still no reply. Priest smiled. "I'm waiting."

All eyes focused upon Hakim, who, with a look of absolute dejection, slowly rose from his chair. With his head bowed, he mumbled that he was.

"Stand up straight, you scumbag, and come to my office right away! Out, now!"

As he was guiding Hakim out of the room, Priest turned to me and said, "If there is any more trouble from anyone send them straight to me at my office. Thank you, Mr Gilbert."

With that he was gone. No incident of that severity happened to me again at Truss. This was because the class, and thereby the school, had seen that I had

Priest's support. Priest was the school's heavy-hitter; he was the terminator.

More kids were frightened of him than anyone else. He knew all the parents in the area, he had been teaching at the school for ten years and he was empowered to exclude pupils – that is, to stop them coming to school for a period of days. Most importantly, he had the respect of the Bengali community who liked his disciplinarian air and forthright manner, so his words carried weight. A call to a parent from John Priest would mean a beating. Priest knew this and had actually been granted permission by many parents to beat their children.

Messing with John Priest had serious consequences. Messing with friends of John Priest also had serious consequences. I had now been officially chalked up as a minor friend; this was enough to enable me to get by in the school without any more major incidents. It didn't mean my life was all chocolate and roses; the kids just knew not to push me too far. Priest didn't bestow this kind of favour upon all teachers; there were some he had no respect for and they had a hell of a time.

# SUPERTEACHER

A major friend of John Priest was Sean Carson, the other English teacher I worked with. The contrast between Sean's classroom and everywhere else in the school was enormous. Every afternoon I would leave the riotous chaos of Figgis's class, dodge past the gum-chewing "raggamuffins" who would "bowl" down the corridor, try not to think about all the smoke coming out of the boys' toilets, push past the meek, cowering Bengali girls in their headscarves and slip into Sean's room.

It was always an oasis of calm and quiet. Sean was one of the few male teachers I've come across who was superb at mounting displays: lavish, colourful diagrams adorned his walls, in each corner there were pot plants and shelves of books, the tables were arranged in little group-work constellations and there was a computer on one of them – a very rare sight in the classrooms of 1991.

Sean had been teaching at the school for twenty years and had previously been a hard-line Marxist. Now he was deeply cynical about all political systems and sneered at most theorists who thought education could instigate the Revolution. He was still quite left-wing though and like most left-wing male teachers was a disciplinarian.

His pep talk to new classes was very short but effective. Most teachers would read through the school's twenty-two point code of conduct as their introduction but Sean didn't bother with any of that.

"I've just got two things to say to this class. I expect you to work and to behave."

That was it. And it appeared to work. The riotous behaviour of other classes just didn't happen. Mind you, Sean was careful not to set himself up for trouble. Despite putting the pupils in groups, he never did any group work. He just liked the aesthetic effect the constellation of desks had upon the classroom. Pupils were either reading or writing. There was no room for directed talk; Sean had no truck with that. In his view, the kids would just muck around.

His lessons had a deeply soporific effect upon me. After the manic intensity of Figgis's ranting and his classes' raging, Sean's lessons were like entering a relaxation chamber. On more than a few occasions I would find myself nodding off as he read softly to the class.

Sean taught the same texts every year. After I had been at the school for a couple of years, I could tell the time of year and day just by being in his lessons; he did the school project with Year 9 in October, he read *A View From The Bridge* with Year 10 in January, *Romeo and Juliet* in March, *Of Mice and Men* in May and so on. Amidst the social turbulence of inner-city London, he had built a timeless world of peace. Everyone in the school yearned for his "control". He was the role model. How did he do it?

He looked the part. He had shaved grey hair, a cowboy moustache and eagle-like blue eyes that were always anticipating, anticipating, anticipating. He saw trouble before it happened and would smooth it over with either a conciliatory gesture or a gentle warning.

He also had a direct hotline to John Priest. He didn't bother with the "On Call" system if there was a problem with a kid. Any real troublemaker was out of his class straight away and having a friendly chat with Priest in his cigar-smokey office.

But most importantly, he had experience on his side. He had clocked up years and years in the school. His reputation went before him; kids knew what to expect a year before they entered his classroom. He had the same sort of presence in the school that a guru might have with his followers; he was talked about with hushed, admiring reverence. Outside the bleak wire fences of Truss he was just an ordinary bloke, but inside he was the Man With A Majorly Successful Plan; he was a kind of shaman, a witch doctor whose influence filtered through the corridors and the years.

Sean was very fit and used the school as his personal gym. He arrived at 6.30am in the morning and went swimming, worked out on the weight machines and went running.

From 7.45am to 8.00am he would sit in the smokers' corner of the staffroom and catch up with the gossip. From 8.00 am to 8.30am he would help kids with their coursework or hold his detentions – if he had any – then he would register his form and begin teaching.

At break he would sit in smokers' corner and have a laugh but during lunch-time he was nearly always helping kids with work and would stay in his class-room, choosing to eat his healthy packed lunch there.

At 3.30pm he was out of the door. One of the great things about working at Truss was that there was very little marking to do – the kids wrote in bite-sized portions. Also, because support teachers like me usually worked on a one-to-one basis with most of the kids who were doing the really important stuff like coursework, so that it was nearly always carefully marked.

We weren't strictly speaking supposed to do this, but teachers like Sean much preferred us to help the average to high ability kids with their work rather than bother with what were considered the "no hopers" – the real ESL kids.

## BOTTOM OF THE LEAGUE TABLES

Nor can I blame Sean for this attitude, because increasingly a culture of putting results before pupils was entering the school system.

In my first year at Truss the first school league tables were published. Truss came bottom of every single school in the country with a measly three per cent of pupils gaining five or more A-C grades at GCSE. A ghastly silence consumed the staffroom that day; the kids seemed to be oblivious to their fate but the teachers weren't.

For the first time in my life, I felt the sensation that I was on the losing side, that there was a terrible sadness in all of this and if I wasn't careful it would engulf me.

# PANTOMIME

After a few days off, Figgis returned to school a rejuvenated person. He'd evidently gone shopping because he was not wearing his regulation punky T-shirt and silver winkle-pickers but was dressed very smartly in an oatmeal suit and open-necked shirt. He was the only person who refused to be glum about the school being officially recognised as the worst in England. He slapped his fist into the palm of his hand and pretended to be overjoyed.

"We're like Millwall, we're the worst team in the world but we're hard!"

"But don't you think that it's all a bit demoralising?" I inquired.

"What do results matter when there is the pantomime to worry about? I've finished it!"

He waved a scruffy handwritten manuscript about in his hands and then, rolling it up into a cone, pointed it at me: "And I've decided to give you the starring role. You're Buttons! You're going to be the lowly school cleaner who gets turned into the head teacher! My plot is absolutely brilliant and you've got all of the lines."

I hesitated. I wasn't sure that I really wanted to have such a prominent role. Figgis prodded me with his manuscript. "You don't realise, Francis, that there is this thing called the Truss Book Of Fate which the Headmistress keeps in a very dusty cupboard in her office. In that book, everything that will happen in this school and has happened has been written down. I know for a fact that your name is written down there; she told me. It was decreed when the stars were set in the sky that you should play this role."

I stared at him in bewilderment. I had never heard a persuasive speech like this before. "The Truss Book Of Fate?"

"So you'll do it?" Figgis said peering at me with wide, Dr-Who eyes.

"Evidently I have no choice in the matter."

"Exactly!" Figgis said with a big grin. "You'll come to learn that there is no such thing as free will in schools. Every school has their own Book Of Fate and what happens in them has to happen. The only thing one can do to ameliorate this sad state of affairs is to be on good terms with the custodian of the book."

Suddenly I realised what he had been up to during all those traumatic lessons when he had sat scribbling at his desk. Figgis nodded vigorously when I told him. "You thought I was being your typical slack teacher, but I wasn't. I knew I was an instrument of fate and had no choice but to write the school pantomime because the Head had told me it was written down in the Truss Book Of Fate!"

## REHEARSALS

The pantomime consumed the attention of most of the staff until the end of term. Figgis had given a role to nearly everyone except for Sean who, because he always disappeared at 3.30pm, wasn't able to attend rehearsals. A festive atmosphere infected the school but it didn't stop us teaching; it just made us more relaxed.

Having taught in many other schools, I have come to realise that there are kids who you can just tell to get on with something if you don't have much of a lesson prepared but you could never, ever do that at Truss. The kids had to be fully occupied at all times; they would have been at each other's throats otherwise.

So the teachers continued working hard but not quite in the same lugubrious way as before. Now there was an ultimate goal to everything; there was a real point. At the end of the day, the staff would file into the theatre laughing and joking about how absurd the thing would look to the kids. Figgis would then sweep in carrying lots of extra photocopied scripts in case people had forgotten theirs. Then he would begin shouting.

He was a highly temperamental director. If someone forgot their lines he would shout at them, "Look at the bloody script! That's not what it says!" The tough teachers – the smokers' brigade lot – would deliberately forget their lines just so that they could laugh at Figgis shouting at them but the other members of the staff, myself included, made damn sure we knew our stuff.

Colin became Figgis's *bête noire*. Colin played one of the Ugly Brothers intent upon stopping Buttons from going to the ball. Figgis had carefully written out a whole load of lines that were exact quotes from films that starred Bob Hoskins – who Colin looked remarkably like. These quotes were lost even on the most film-literate of the staff and didn't really fit in with the play, so Colin started to improvise. Figgis got progressively more and more enraged until he burst into tears on the day before the performance. It was at this point, much to the merriment of the other staff, that Colin finally remembered his lines.

# THE LAST DAY OF TERM

Sharon Day's hands were shaking. She was my Princess Charming; the one who would sweep me off my feet at the end of the show. Figgis had decided to write a feminist pantomime where the woman, not the man, was the saviour.

Sharon looked furtively around the staffroom and then pulled out a whisky bottle from her bag. I was shocked. Sharon was not the kind of person you'd expect to be carrying around a half-empty whisky bottle in her trendy, glittery bag; she was a good looking woman in her mid-thirties who wore tight fitting skirts and tops. She was Head of Year 11 which basically meant that she was in charge of making sure the nasty kids in that year behaved in lessons and around the school. As far as I could see, she was pretty successful at this. She jiggled about in high heels, charming even the most horrible bullies into being moderately pleasant.

She swigged at the bottle and indicated that I should do the same. Suddenly she was making me nervous. I took a gulp. Sharon quickly squirrelled the bottle back into her bag and put her hand on my arm.

"That feels better, doesn't it?" I nodded. Before I

knew where I was, I had agreed with her to go to her office and we were between us polishing off the bottle in her tiny, secluded cubby-hole on the third floor of the main building.

"I should have never have agreed to do this blasted pantomime," Sharon said. "I get terrible stage fright. I can't even face taking the tube to work, such is my fear of enclosed spaces."

"But the stage isn't an enclosed space," I commented.

"No. I suppose it isn't," Sharon hiccupped.

"But Figgis makes you feel like it is!"

We laughed uproariously at this. The whisky fizzed around my veins, making me feel giddy. I was shut up in a tiny room with a very attractive woman in a tight top and I was already feeling quite drunk. The bell went for registration before I could reach over to her and kiss her on her cherry lips. I slouched off to my form whom I shared with Colin. Luckily, Colin took the register because I was in no state to read Bengali names off the page at that point.

Then Colin and I disappeared to the theatre, leaving the class with a cover teacher. Once backstage we quickly changed and waited for the kids to fill up the hall. Figgis was in an exceptionally jolly mood, spurring on his troops. He hadn't noticed at that point that his lead actor was totally pissed.

I can't remember that much about my performance, apart from the fact that I forgot every single one of my lines but somehow managed to carry on. Afterwards I was told by the staff who were watching that the performance was far funnier than anything that Figgis had written because I simplified everything; all the subtle puns and references were thrown out of the window and replaced by a crude, rude and stumbling pantomime. I can remember the kids roaring with laughter.

However, that said, I realise now that the kids would have laughed at anything we did. Even through my drunken haze, I sensed, in a way that I had never had before, that they were on our side. For all their truculence, they liked us. Out of the corner of my eye I could see Jafar and Hakim laughing with us and the whole of 9A cheering us on.

Once I had been rescued from the evil clutches of the Ugly Brother by Princess Charming and the school had applauded uproariously and been dismissed, the staff crawled to the staffroom where nearly half of us started dancing to the tunes of the 1970s which were played on a tinny boom-box sitting on the mouldy fridge. Still quite oblivious to the difficulties I had caused in the play by forgetting all my lines, I danced joyously with Sharon; it was the end of term! I was free! It was the holidays! The pupils had cheered at me!

I was in such an ecstatic mood that even Figgis couldn't be cross with me.

"I guess it was all written in the Truss Book Of Fate," he said to me, somewhat mournfully. At the time, I couldn't understand his rueful tone but the next morning, suffering from a bad hangover, I did. Luckily, it was the holidays and I wouldn't have to face him for a couple of weeks.

## CLEANING WINDOWS

We returned to school in the dead of winter and taught, with a week's break in February, right into spring. Whereas in my first term my timetable had felt fundamentally mysterious and unknowable, now I knew it off by heart. I didn't have to look at my teacher's planner to know what I would be doing at any given time in the week. I measured my life by those four blocks of time that now stood immovably in the centre of each day like a series of buildings of varying sizes. I felt like a window cleaner who had to scrub the windows of my classes clean; I had to elucidate the English language for them, to make it transparent, to make it shine.

***

Some windows were much easier to clean than others. On Mondays, I would slouch into work because not only did I have a whole week's worth of windows to clean with some very meagre materials but I also had the hardest building to clean last thing that day and on Friday last thing as well – 9A. The thought of having to deal with them increasingly filled me with dread. I felt as though their windows were broken and that I could get my hands cut at any time.

The other classes were easy in comparison. Teaching Year 7 drama periods one and two was not difficult; I taught with another teacher, Pam Drabble, who was very experienced. She taught in an isolated building that was separate from the school; the room was not heated properly and the kids' breath plumed in the air as they ran around the room. They had to take their shoes off in the room; gazing at their socks made me aware of just how poor these children were. They nearly all wore threadbare socks and some had none at all.

They loved drama. Pam's firm hand made them feel safe, but also confident enough to express themselves. She was an earthy, working-class woman with quite a brash but friendly manner. She would start the lesson with a game, usually traffic lights or statues. They would run around the room and then stop if she shouted red, run on the spot if she said amber and leap into action once she said green. With statues she would ask them to make different shapes – a cow, a building, a tree – and then freeze! They were very simple games but the kids loved them.

With the main part of the lesson, Pam would choose a topic which would stretch over a couple of weeks and ask the pupils in groups to come up with an improvised play based on that topic. While I was at the school, we covered just about everything from fairytales to bullying, from Shakespeare to immigration. Pam would always structure the lessons so that each group would do things in very carefully defined stages: brainstorm ideas, allocate roles, talk about the characters, plan the plot and then improvise. The groups would then perform their role plays to the class and get feedback, so that they could improve it for a final performance to which they would bring costumes and music.

I would work with the language learners, helping them in their groups. I would join in with their plays and act with them. It was great fun.

*\*\**

There was an issue at this time about whether the school should continue employing a drama teacher because there were concerns about the budget and drama wasn't a subject on the National Curriculum. This meant that the school wasn't obliged by law to provide drama lessons.

It would have been a terrible loss if the school had got rid of Pam. Fortunately, the Deputy Head realised this and invited the Chief Inspector in the authority to observe a lesson I taught with Pam. The inspector noted that the kids probably learnt more language in their drama lesson than in all the other lessons combined.

Teaching English within those drama lessons was like polishing up the windows of a lovely, cosy cottage. The physical environment which we worked in may have been appalling but we inhabited a higher spiritual sphere there; the children were enfolded by red plush chairs and a well tended house and were probably having the happiest experiences of their school lives – for some, perhaps the whole of their lives. I can still see, in my mind's eye, the delight of a tiny girl, April Pearman, as she played the wicked witch in Pam's modernised version of *Snow White*.

After lessons one and two, there was a break when Pam and I would return to the school, talking about how the lesson had gone. It was always the middle of break by the time we got back because our lessons would inevitably overrun. I would grab a slice of pizza from the tea lady who set up stall during break times, and would sit down next to Figgis who had become my staffroom buddy. He nearly always made a joke about my eating habits like, "Live long, eat healthy" or comment, "You look as bad as I feel," and together we would laugh uneasily.

I never felt truly relaxed in his company but I was pleased he wanted to be my friend. Truss had a backbone of long-standing staff – people like Figgis and Pam had been at the school for at least five years – but there were always new faces, mostly temporary teachers who were generally shunned by the more senior time-servers[3]. I fell into the category of temporary staff and so it was quite unusual that a person like Figgis was taking an interest in me.


## THE BUILDING SITE

After break, I would join Figgis with his Year 11. The longer I taught at Truss the more I came to appreciate Figgis's techniques. His lessons were a perpetual building site. He always had some new

---

3.<u>Staffroom hierarchies</u>: Schools are incredibly hierarchical places. They are structured in a rather feudal way. The Head is at the top and has all the important powers like the ability to grant you leave if you need it and the right to write your reference if you are looking for another job. The Deputy Head is next in line, followed by other senior staff who do things like arrange the timetable. Heads of Department and Heads of Year are next and are supported by their deputies. Near the bottom of the ladder are the lowly mainstream teachers, followed by the support teachers who truly languish in the pit of this hierarchy.

Truss was quite unusual in that it had its own alternative hierarchy. In it there was an upper class of teachers who had "respect": Sean Carson was the undisputed king and his courtiers were teachers like Pam Drabble, Colin and a couple of others from smokers corner. Slightly below them were characters like Figgis and Sharon Day who may not have had the control over the kids that the king and courtiers had but were nevertheless increasingly forces to be reckoned with. And then there was the rest of us followed by the "balm pots" and the "nutters".

idea under construction and he involved me in the building work thoroughly. I was always much more than a window cleaner in his lessons. I was never bored. He kept trying new things.

During that term, Figgis invented a unit of work called "*EastEnders*: myth and reality". This involved showing his class a few episodes of *EastEnders* and getting them to analyse the plot-lines of the show, the characters and the themes. Figgis then asked the class to think of the characters living in their own neighbourhood and to write about them. The class then filled individual charts trying to match the characters in the TV show with their real-life counterparts. Finally, the class, after quite a bit of discussion, wrote an essay about whether *EastEnders* reflected the reality of their own lives.

The whole exercise brought home to me just what a miserable sham of a show *EastEnders* was. It had absolutely nothing to do with these kids' lives; it was about as much a reflection of their lives as *Dallas* was. I was surprised about how resigned the kids were about this; there was a sadness in the way they would say to me that they couldn't expect anyone to write about their lives.

Quite a few kids saw the work as just another piece

of school work, but a couple didn't. One of these was Hakim. As the lessons progressed he seemed to become more and more involved in the work; he stopped jeering and sniggering at Figgis, stopped making silly jokes and got out his pen and wrote. I read his essay. It was clear that he was very angry.

"No one is interested in the Bengalis in England. *EastEnders* is a joke. It has no Bengali people in it. It has Indians in it but they are not the sort of Indians who live in the East End," he said to me. "It pretends to be about the East End but it is a lie. Why are we always ignored? All that happens is that we get grief; the police cuss us, the white people cuss us, they make us go to shit schools and live in shit flats."

I tried to calm him down by saying that it was up to him to change things, to get his qualifications and to write a new and better TV show that would tell the truth. But this seemed to depress him. He waved me away with his hand. "I'm not going to get anything here. You know that. Don't say this shit to me," he said bitterly.

These words scorched me and I left him alone to write his furious piece.

# SOME INFAMOUS CHARACTERS

The last lesson of the day is always the worst. Especially when it has been raining at lunch-time. And it always seemed to be raining during that dark term. 9A always seemed to be sodden and raucous and bellicose when I encountered them. By now, I knew a great deal about every single kid in that class. The major criminals were:

Yumni. He had a pleasant, smiley face and had something of the demeanour of Mickey Mouse on speed. He was forever jumping up and down and found it impossible to sit in his seat. I tried to be friendly with him. This was a mistake because he would greet me by offering me a high five or, if my back was turned and Colin was out of the room, by slapping the back of my head. This was something I should have done something about, but it all felt quite jokey and I was ashamed to admit the problem to any other teacher. He usually did his work once he was settled down and I felt that enduring such greetings was part of the trade off.

Bilal was the really brainy kid in the class. He was sallow-faced and rather sinister. He would like to ask me awkward questions about my private life. "Have

116

you ever had sex, sir? When did you last do it? What tips would you give me about going out with a girl?" And so on. He was a good writer and wrote weird tales about strange happenings on space stations. At a parents' evening, I complained to his father about his cheekiness. His Dad didn't speak much English and became quite annoyed. "You can't control him? What the matter with you? You got problems, big problems!" I backed down and said that his rudeness wasn't a major problem and this calmed his Dad down, at which point he said, "You get any more problems, tell me. I got this system. We put Bilal in the bath and then put bricks on him. He behaves after that."

Needless to say I never complained to his father about Bilal's lippiness after hearing this.

Shadi was the class drug dealer and was a very scary character. Fortunately, he rarely came into lessons but when he did it was nearly impossible to get any work done because the boys crowded around him listening to him tell tales about the gang fights he had been involved in. Shadi was a leading member of the Brick Lane Massive, a gang of kids who spent most of their time drug-running and fighting the Cannon Street Massive.

I never got a grip on the class during that first year.

We finished reading *Friend or Foe* and then I felt at a loss about what to do with them, so we read an abridged version of *Dracula*; it took me the whole of the Christmas term and Spring term to read these two short books with them. I spent so much time writing worksheets for them to keep them occupied that I never got much reading done.


## SPRING


Classrooms were brighter in the mornings; sunlight would occasionally dapple the top of the Canary Wharf tower, seagulls would swoop in and out of the playground, the odd child would flash me a well-meaning smile, the cussing and fighting seemed to abate a little.

However, it was becoming clear that I might fail my probationary year if 9A didn't improve. Tom Hardy had been into my lessons a few times more and hadn't particularly liked what he had seen, despite my efforts to do group work with the kids. "You're not differentiating enough with them. You haven't established any meaningful learning patterns with them," he would say.

I explained my dilemma to Colin who continued to support the class with me. "I think Hardy is wrong. You're doing a great job, Francis. Don't listen to him. I think the school is letting you down. No one is helping you out. You're being left to the wolves and they are running tonight," Colin said. Then, rubbing his prickly chin, he mused, "Listen, I'll have a word with John Priest and see if he can do anything for you. He helped you out with Figgis's class, didn't he?"

## THE PRIEST IS SENT FOR

9A knew it was serious this time. For the first time ever, there was silence when I entered the room. They could see who was behind me – the chunky, dour form of John Priest smelling of cigars and discipline. He paced into the room in his black suit like Darth Vader and walked up and down the classroom as he said, "I have been hearing things about this class that I don't like."

He strolled past Yumni and stopped and stared. Yumni looked sheepish and silly in an oversized Donald Duck cap that he always brought out in my lessons; I was forever asking him to take it off. Without a word,

Yumni quickly pulled the ridiculous headgear off his head and stuffed it into his bag. Priest did this with a few of the other kids; just staring at them without saying anything and waiting for them to adjust their uniform so that it met the school's constantly flouted regulations.

At this point, Colin slipped into the room at his customary late hour. Priest eyed him suspiciously. For some unknown reason, Priest didn't like Colin. Priest then said, "I know many of your parents well. Many of them have given me permission to beat you. Don't mess around any more, 9A, or you might be heading that way."

With that, Priest swept out of the room. There was a stunned silence for a few moments. I was able to explain the main objectives of the lesson without being interrupted but gradually, like the sun shining upon an icy stream of water, the class thawed and soon talk and mischief were spilling out of them in their usual fashion. Only this time, I was no longer their soft-hearted friend but a potential Priest spy; someone to be despised.

Yumni said, "What you get him in for? He ain't no good. We're your mates sir, you shouldn't have done that!"

"You're not my mates, you're my pupils," I responded.

"We're not your mates now," Yumni said, retrieving his ratty Donald Duck cap and plonking it on his head.

"Yumni, take that off now!" I said.

"And what? You're going to send me for a beating?"

I hesitated. Yumni was a clever kid; he may not have written anything all year but he had sussed out my moral apparatus. He knew that I wouldn't do that.

"Just take off the hat," I said.

"OK," he said but kept the hat on and grinned.

I walked away from him to attend to another pupil. At the time, I thought of this as a victory of sorts because he may not have taken the cap off his head but he had sort of conceded the necessity of doing so. But now, I can see how Priest's comments had corrupted the discourse I had with the class; before his arrival I had been honest with them. Now we had to pretend we were keeping to school rules but we were continuing exactly as before. I realise now that this is what Priest wanted. He didn't want to hear the truth about my rowdy lessons; he wanted me to pretend that everything was fine.[4]

"He's an idiot," Colin said to me as we walked back to the staffroom after the lesson. "He thinks he's hard but he's just a total idiot. What he said then was nothing short of criminal. Abusive. He's got some serious psychological problems."

The venom in Colin's words shocked me; his friendly, avuncular tone had gone entirely and was replaced by a hissing, tight-fisted poison. He hated Priest.

## HAKIM DISAPPEARS

Hakim hadn't been spotted in school for ages. This was particularly a shame for Figgis and me because he only had one piece of work to be completed in order to finish his English coursework. He was one of the few candidates who was likely to get a C grade. Figgis was busy marking the coursework before it was sent off to the exam board and so asked me to look into Hakim's absences.

4.Appearance and reality: Most schools that are poorly run are obsessed with keeping up appearances and positively discourage their staff to tell the truth about what is going on in the lessons. Staff who say that they are having difficulties are ridiculed or made to feel inadequate and basically told to put up or shut up. Truss was a relatively honest school; most staff were willing to tell the truth about their classes.

I went to see Sharon Day, the Head of Year 11 and the person who was ultimately responsible for Hakim's welfare in school. I hadn't spoken to Sharon Day properly since the pantomime. Now it was early May. A cool, summery breeze swept through the corridor as I made my way to her office.

Smiling gently, she listened to me talk about Hakim in a tight-fitting top. It was quite distracting but I managed to tell her the salient points. She leaned forward and touched my hand, "You care, don't you Francis?"

For some reason, I found this quite a moving comment. I gulped. It hadn't dawned upon me for quite a while why I was doing all of this. Sharon let go of my hand and picked up a pencil, "I think we need to pay Hakim a visit; his mother doesn't have a phone so we'll have to go to his home. And it's a good thing we are because I want you and me to check out another home right next door. You are staying on next year, aren't you?"

This question caught me by surprise. I hadn't seriously considered what I was going to do next year. I nodded weakly. Sharon clapped her hands together. "Good, good. Because I want you to be one of my form tutors. I'm going to be in charge of Year 7 next year, the new intake, and I would love you to be part of my team."

## HOME VISITS

After school, Sharon and I strolled out into the streets of Stepney. There were abundant blossoms on the grimy trees in the graveyard of St Anthony's Church. Outside the Caribbean cafe off Shakespeare Road a couple of guys were playing chess, and in the launderette a number of grim-faced, headscarved wives were watching their washing. We moved beyond these relatively sociable surroundings and found ourselves in a very inhospitable council estate. Our shoes crunched over broken bottles and a ripped-up pornographic magazine. We entered a dark stairwell and I began to feel nervous. Sharon told me not to worry; she'd visited this block quite a few times before and had never had any trouble.

We found Hakim's flat on the fourth floor. Sharon knocked. At first there was no answer, but she kept trying and eventually we heard footsteps. The door was opened on a chain and a wrinkled, ageing woman with a black scarf covering her face peered up at us.

"Is Hakim there?" Sharon asked but received no reply. She then said a few words in Bengali and this evinced a brief response. The wrinkled mother shook her head. Sharon sighed. She whispered that she was certain Hakim was there but the mother was covering for him.

Then Sharon surprised me by shouting over the mother, "Hakim, we know you're home. You're not in trouble. We just want to talk to you!"

This caused the lady to scuttle away into the bowels of the flat, leaving the door open. Sharon pushed the door open further, explaining that the mother had said we could come in. The flat was a bleak affair. There were no carpets and virtually no furniture. But I was surprised to see a large brand-new TV sitting on the floor in the spartan front room. Languishing before its jabbering light, lying propped up against the wall on a mound of cloth, was Hakim. His mother went and sat in front of a large sewing-machine besides which were stacked a large tower of cloth squares. A smell of rancid fat pervaded the room.

"Hakim, we were worried about you. You haven't been in school in weeks," Sharon said.

Hakim didn't stop looking at the TV as he answered, "Gotta help my mum. Been too busy."

"But Hakim, you've got your GCSEs coming up. Mr Gilbert here thinks you can do well in your English if you only finish one piece of coursework."

I nodded in agreement. Hakim looked up and fixed me in the eyes.

"How can I work for someone who insulted my mum?" he said.

This comment startled me. At first, I didn't know what he was talking about and then I remembered. "That was ages ago, Hakim. Are you still upset about that?" I asked.

Hakim didn't reply. Sharon glanced at me, looking puzzled. I explained to her that Hakim had been kicked out of the class a few months ago and then Mr Figgis had made a joke that could have been taken the wrong way.

"Hakim, you can't let this little thing get in the way of your future. We want you to do well, Hakim. We know you can. But you have to finish your studies. We care about you. We wouldn't have gone to all this effort otherwise," Sharon said. "You could write for TV and not watch it all the time if you tried. I can really see you doing that." These last words softened Hakim's tense features. Sharon knew Hakim. She knew that this was his dream.

"Do you think?" he asked, peering up at her with hopeful eyes.

"But you need to get your GCSEs first," Sharon said in a soothing tone.

***

Hakim walked out with us, promising that he would come to school the next day — a promise which he kept and which ultimately ensured that he successfully completed his GCSEs. We left him at the edge of the estate.

We crossed the road and entered another grim precinct. The flats here were far worse than Hakim's estate; many of the windows on the lower floors were either boarded up or broken. The buildings were also configured in such a way so that there was no light anywhere, just a thick gloom. Sharon knocked on a door; it swung open quickly and a little girl appeared in the doorway.

"Hello, Shahana. Do you remember me? I came and visited you at your school. You are not at our school yet, but you will be in September. We wanted to pay you a visit before you joined us at Peter Truss. I'm Ms Day and this is Mr Gilbert. He's going to be your new form tutor. We were just visiting someone else and we thought we would call on you too."

The girl seemed very shy. She put her arm over her eyes, but she was smiling.

An overpowering smell of rubbish seemed to be emanating from the innards of the flat; if Hakim's flat had been bleak, this place looked desperate. I could see that the walls were damp and seemed to be crawling with black insects. A big, unshaven man lumbered into view and hovered over Shahana.

"Hello, Mr Uddin," Sharon said, unperturbed by his somewhat menacing presence. "How are you?"

He pulled Shahana away from the door and gesticulated with his arms.

"When you get us out of here? Look, cockroaches. Cockroaches everywhere," he said.

"We're not from the council, Mr Uddin. We're from Shahana's new school. I wanted to introduce Shahana's new tutor to her. My name is Ms Day," Sharon said.

"When you get us out? Get us out!" he shouted.

Sharon backed away and said that it was time for us to go now but that we would see Shahana and him soon. Mr Uddin watched us leave, still shouting that he needed to get out. It was quite an unnerving experience. He didn't really seem to be conscious of who we were; his eyes were glazed and slightly runny. He had very red eyes. Worse than mine at their worst.

As we walked back, Sharon explained to me the situation with Shahana. The social services were very worried about her. She was on the "At Risk Register" because her social worker believed she was being severely neglected. Her parents were from Yemen and were initially from the desert where they had lived a primitive and nomadic life. Now they had refugee status here. Sharon had taught Shahana's brothers and had met Mr Uddin several times but his memory was so bad that he hadn't remembered her. The social services thought that he mght be schizophrenic. He had seven other children apart from Shahana.

"I'll arrange for you to meet Shahana's Educational Welfare Officer. Shahana has special educational needs on top of everything else and so has an Educational Welfare Officer as well as a social worker. All the agencies are on Shahana's case," Sharon said.

We returned to school, talking about all of the problems in the area: the poverty, the lack of opportunities, the cycle of abuse that meant that all the troubles of the previous generation were passed on to the next. It was depressing, but talking to Sharon made me feel that something could be done about it.

I was very pleased to be one of her form tutors.

## PROBATION

But before I could become a form tutor, I had to pass my probation. Everything hinged upon a final lesson observation. Tom Hardy had told me that he needed to see significant evidence of improvement regarding differentiation and involving the pupils in group work.

In late June, the dreaded English adviser sat in the back of my lesson with the sun streaming in through the windows on the upper floor of the building. Outside, in the deep blue sky there was a glorious sense of freedom and summer, but inside I felt trapped. I really, really wanted to pass my probation; I wanted to be part of Sharon's team, wanted to be a fully-fledged teacher. Despite all my difficulties, I felt as though I could make a good teacher.

Fortunately for me – although I didn't realise it at the time – Tom Hardy plonked himself in the middle of a group which consisted of the naughtiest boys in the class: Yumni, Bilal, Uthman and Bulus. I was surprised by his choice of seat because he normally preferred to sit at the back of the class with his clipboard.

We were doing something called 'The Island Project'. This was a unit of work that had been dragging on for weeks because the kids seemed to be quite into it. Every group in the class had to invent an island which they were marooned on and had to write diaries, reports, newspaper articles and survival guides for their island. For this lesson, I had decided to read a section of *Robinson Crusoe* where he finds Man Friday, and ask the pupils to imagine that they find a stranger on the island and to write about it. Then, one member in each group would go to another group and tell them about their strangers, reading out sections of their diaries to them. The lesson would end with a whole class feedback which would focus upon the kinds of language needed to describe a stranger. I had written four different worksheets for the lesson: a simple fill-in-the-blanks sheet and comic strip for the ESL learners, a more advanced fill-in-the-blanks for the pupils who were fractionally better than these characters and a more complicated instruction sheet for the able children, i.e. Yumni, Bilal, Uthman and Bulus.

The lesson went well. The pupils listened to my reading of *Robinson Crusoe*, listened to my instructions and merrily got on with writing their diaries. They all used the verbs and adjectives I had talked about using: shocked, mysterious, unknown, etc.

Tom Hardy tried to muck in with his group but was rebuffed by Yumni, "Why don't you shut up, man. Us geezers here are doing it for ourselves!"

The rest of the group sniggered at this. Bilal asked the adviser whether he had ever considered wearing a wig and Uthman speculated to Bulus whether Hardy wanted any gear. They were giving him a right turning-over until I approached the table and asked them how the project was going; they hadn't done much but with me helping them they started writing.

This was truly a miracle, but the group and I tried to make out that this was just what happened in every lesson. I shivered. It was amazing. These kids were on my side. They knew that I was being checked out and they wanted to help me. They hadn't been much help in the previous lessons when Hardy had visited but now, when it came to the crunch, they were batting for me.

At the end of the lesson, Hardy nodded grimly at me. He didn't make any comment. He said he had an appointment with the Head and that I should follow him. My heart was pounding as we walked down the stairs and along the corridor to the Head's office. What was going on? Was Hardy going to fail me after that lesson? Perhaps those boys' cheekiness had got to him. Perhaps he was going to fail me after all.

I felt that I would protest if he did. That lesson had it all: variety, pace, challenging material, pupils who were on task. The injustice of it!

I waited outside the Head's office as Hardy entered. I stood there for about ten agonising minutes before being ushered in by Hardy himself. I was all ready to defend myself but immediately I could tell from the Headmistress's lopsided smile that I had passed. She told me to sit down and then said, "Well, Francis, I have just signed this document here which says that you are a fully-qualified teacher. Tom and I would like to congratulate you upon what has turned out to be a very good year. Well done!"

She stood up and shook my hand. I beamed at her. Then Hardy shook my hand limply.

"You have done well considering the lack of resources in your department," Hardy said. "In most schools in the borough you would have been supported a great deal better than you have been here."

"Yes, yes, well, I don't think this is the time or the place for all of this," the Headmistress interrupted. "I'll make sure that Joe sits down with Francis and they work out a good curriculum for his classes next year."

With these words, she virtually shooed Hardy and me out of her office and into the corridor. I faced him as he turned to go. Suddenly, I had the feeling that he had been far more on my side than I had ever suspected. He'd been playing a game of double bluff. He had wanted to frighten me so that I would make the extra effort and because he wanted the English department to improve.

These thoughts were confirmed a week later when Joe Dicey sought me out and talked to me about what I might teach next year. Dicey seemed particularly dejected. He rubbed his eyes and scratched his white beard as he said, "There was never any question of him failing you. We all know you're a good teacher. Hardy just wants to get at me. He thinks that I am running things poorly here and he's probably right. This job is so different from what it used to be. When I first started it was all white working-class children and they hadn't seen a TV, video or computer game, so the moment you put a decent book in front of them, a lot of them wanted to learn. And that's what you did. You read literature with them. Read them good stories. Now that's all gone out of the window with all this differentiation and group-work stuff."

I listened to him talk in this nostalgic vein for a while and soon realised that there was no way he was going to help me structure my curriculum for next year for the simple reason that he just didn't know how to.

No one was more delighted that I had passed my probation than Colin. He bought me a chocolate bar and a cup of tea the next day at break. He laughed jovially at all my worries about failing and then said, "Listen, why don't you bring 9A for a weekend to my house in Norfolk? They would love it and it would be a chance for you to bond even more with them before you take them on to next year."

I stopped biting into my chocolate bar at this point. Much as I had come to like 9A, I wasn't sure that I liked them enough to spend a whole weekend in their company.

"Yeah, maybe, maybe... someday," I said rather dubiously.

Colin didn't particularly like this reply. "You might actually get to know them if you spent a bit more time with them."

"We can't all be as devoted to our classes as you," I quipped. I was aware that Colin regularly took his own form away for trips during the weekends. He usually got a member from smokers' corner to come with him, but this time he was asking me.

I felt a little ashamed of myself going home that day because I knew that I would never be as devoted to my classes as Colin was. I wanted my weekends to myself. I didn't want to adopt the children in my classes. I wanted to do my best teaching them but I knew now that I could never be their saviour. One year at Truss had wised me up to myself; there were definite limits to my charity.

## STARTING OVER

"Now 7Q, I need you to listen very carefully. In this school, you behave. You do not talk when a teacher is talking. Can anyone tell me why?"

It is the first day back in September. Sunlight floods into the classroom illuminating all its manifold imperfections: chiselled graffiti, scuffed walls, battered cupboard doors, a dusty old blackboard. Before me are twenty-nine eleven-year-olds sitting quivering in their oversized uniforms. I can feel their fear and I am thriving on it. I know that I have to make the most of it before they lose it completely. I need to show them that I am a frightening guy when disobeyed.

A small black girl whose parents are from Sierra Leone puts up her hand. "Yes, Grace, why must we never talk when the teacher is talking?"

Grace grins. "Because you must always listen to your teacher."

"Very good. Now can anyone think why we must never chew gum in lessons?"

But Grace hasn't finished. "But what I want to know is: what if there is a fire and it's burning your pants. Are you allowed to talk without permission then?"

Most other classes would have sniggered at this comment, but not this one. Grace seems to be the only one intent upon having fun. I know all about her. She is a very bright girl who caused a great deal of trouble in her primary school. She is someone who is already challenging my authority.

But this is my opportunity to prove myself.

"Stand up now, Grace!" I shout furiously. I feel the whole class freeze in their seats. Grace's big, naughty eyes swivel in their sockets and fix upon the desk before her, assiduously avoiding my gaze. She stands up. "Did I ask you to speak? Did I?" I bawl at her.

"No sir," she says meekly.

"Don't do it again. And that goes for all of you," I say modulating into a soft voice. "Sit down!"

She sits down in silence without a smirk upon her face and I continue with my lecture about the school rules. Oh, just look at me! How different I am from last year! I prowl the classroom like the King Of Cats teaching his cubs. I have got a bit of every teacher I respect within my veins: I have got Sean Carson's trick of suddenly shouting at the right moment, of inspiring fear, I have got Pam Drabble's ability to spell out rules and explain things ultra clearly, I have got a little of Figgis's jokiness and creativity, I have got a little of Cynthia James's theatricality.

Or at least this is how it feels at the time. It's a confidence that I will lose as the year progresses but I have it in abundance at this point. Besides which, I am even beginning to look the part. Gone is the long, greasy hair; now it is cropped short and mean and clean like Sean's. Gone are the Paisley shirts; more sober checked shirts have replaced them. Gone are the scruffy jeans; I wear smart black ones. Gone are the battered Desert Boots; I wear regularly buffed-up Doctor Martens. I have got a new girlfriend – who will soon become my wife – and a whole year of experience. And it shows.

As I talk to my new form about their future life in the school, I enjoy, for the first time ever, an enormous sensation of power. I know more about this institution than these kids, a lot more. I feel as though I can use this place to my advantage; to shape and mould these children into Gilbert children. They will carry the stamp of me for the rest of their lives.

## NEW ROUTINE, NEW MACHINE

This new super-duper-upgraded me took his duties very seriously. My school life now revolved around my form. Every morning I would wake in my flat in King's Cross and flee to the sanctuary of the school; it had become more my home now than my miserable lodgings. I would have breakfast at the school at about seven-thirty and spend the rest of the time preparing for the day ahead. Like Sean, I would go up to my form room at about eight where I would continue with my marking and preparation. Gradually, I would watch the members of my form trickle into the room. Word quickly got round that I was usually in my room from eight and I soon discovered that there were quite a few kids who were only too anxious to get out of the house. Usually most of the form were in the room before eight -thirty; actual registration would start at 8.45am. But it was clear that the pupils liked the sanctuary of the form room; they could get help from me with their homework or could sit and chatter away with their friends in warmth and comfort. I got the pupils to put their own displays in the room, so that by the end of the Christmas term it was a real home from home.

I would then register the form and ask them to get on with silent reading before lessons began at 9am. This enabled me to deal with individual problems. My form had quite a few of those. There was Shahana, whom Sharon Day and I had already visited before she joined the school, with her mentally-ill father living amongst the cockroaches. She had severe learning difficulties and often stank of her terrible flat; kids sitting next to her would complain about the smell. She could barely read and write and I tried to help her with her reading when I could. There was Grace, who was very able but intent upon winding up every one of her teachers with her cheekiness and constant interruptions. There was Nabil who had no stomach and had a colostomy bag and wore nappies. The class had to be told about his medical condition and asked to be patient if there was a funny smell. The kids were surprisingly understanding. He also had learning difficulties and had the writing abilities of a six-year-old.

There was Bashir whose family kept moving from B&B to B&B; he spoke very little English despite having been in the country since he was four. His former primary school marked him out as being a very disruptive and disturbed pupil who had only been there for six months. There were no records further back than that.

And there was Hassan, whose brothers had just left the school to become fully involved in the East End Bengali gangs; he looked like he might go the same way if we weren't careful. He and his sidekick, Fatih, were forever getting into fights or cussing someone or other. They were serious bullies.

After dealing with my form, lessons would begin. Now I had a full timetable and was teaching more English. Unlike last year, I found that there was definite rhythm to each day. Being a more experienced teacher and more used to the school made a difference. I was able to sing-song my way through the first two lessons of the day; they were usually drama lessons or lessons teaching English to my form. I had to work hard in these lessons but I found them interesting and the kids relatively easy to manage.

This would take me up to lunch because the lessons at Truss were always double lessons; the first one being from 9.05am to 10.20, the second being 10.45am to 12.00pm. There was then a break for lunch. The last two lessons of the day were from 12.55pm to 2.10pm and 2.15pm to 3.30pm.

It was these last two lessons which were the killers. For some reason – and this has apparently been scientifically proven to be the case – children are much less able to concentrate after lunch and this was noticeable in their attitude to their learning. I always taught 10A (formerly the infamous 9A) and 9K English after lunch. These were lessons where I was the main English teacher and I was often without support.

My youth and enthusiasm carried me through but life was not without its difficulties. I was, you see, without knowing, well on my way to becoming a controloholic.[5]

## CONTROLOHOLISM

I think I became a controloholic because I had caught glimpses of success; there had been times, for example, when I had been sufficiently on top of really difficult classes to have been able to read to them for forty minutes with them listening in silence. It sounds pathetic that I should have been pleased with myself for this but given the context of the classes I was working with, it was a major victory. There were days now when I was able to talk without being interrupted at the beginning of lessons. Sometimes I could even get the children to work in silence.

In order to do this with challenging classes, a teacher has to be obsessive about maintaining order.

5.<u>Symptoms of controloholism</u>:

a) Being obsessed by noise levels. Checking noise levels like a meteorologist takes the temperature of the air.

b) Having a tendency to say "sssh" a lot under one's breath. Oh my God, how many teachers do I know that seem to "shush" almost spontaneously when confronted with a group of noisy children? It's like Tourette's syndrome with shushing. I know because I am still guilty of this.

c) Being a stickler for tiny details. This is how a real controloholic gets his kicks: making sure that the date is written in the "correct" fashion, shouting at children for not underlining titles, getting worked up about margins and so forth is very effective. The controloholic may not be that interested in the quality of a child's work – usually he/she is too busy controlling to do that – but presentation is an area where a maximum degree of control can be exerted.

d) Feeling a warm glow of pleasure when a class is beavering away in silence.

e) Feeling distinctly agitated if there is too much talking, whether or not it is related to the work.

# ORDER

My growing controloholism led to my getting very impatient with pupils who were threatening to disrupt my "perfectly ordered" classrooms. The odd kid who was chattering quietly as I was reading was a major source of annoyance. In my second year at Truss, I took on 9K, a difficult class which I managed to keep under "control". I read a lot of class readers with them and they sat and listened. It didn't matter that much to me whether they were all understanding that much, what mattered was that I was reading what was on the syllabus and I was reading it quickly with them. I had been stung by Tom Hardy's criticism that I had offered my pupils a thin diet of literature.

In fact, not wanting to repeat the errors of 9A, I decided to read a fantastic number of books with 9K: *The Friends* by Rosa Guy, *Across The Barricades* by Joan Lingard, *The Outsiders* by S.E. Hinton. These are a lot of books for any class to get through in a term but considering that most of the children had reading ages of seven year olds or below, it was phenomenal – or so I thought.

I determined that I was going to punish any little runt who threatened to stop my unstoppable train of reading. However, I was aware that although the pupils appeared to be listening, they might not be. I was conscious that little notes were being passed around the room as I read, that bags were being removed from under desks and shifted around the class. I decided to crush this behaviour out of all existence. One day, I caught a kid who was about to pass someone else's bag under the table. I grabbed him by the arm while continuing to read to the class, pulled him to the front of the classroom, opened the door and threw him out into the corridor. I didn't say anything about it but ploughed on with my reading.

The bag-passing stopped after that. But it gave me a fatal sense of security. It made me think that this sort of silent, physical action was not only all right; it was positively beneficial. I started doing a little more often; grabbing boys by the arms when they were misbehaving – often for quite trivial things – and showing them who was boss.

Because I was increasingly within the loop of staffroom gossip, I learnt that some teachers were committing far worse sins than I was. I never actually hit any children, but there were a few pedagogues whose chosen method of control was cuffing children on the back of the head.

This was how their teachers had treated them, how their parents had treated them; it had worked with them and it worked at Truss. Very few kids actually complained. They knew their parents wouldn't be understanding and probably would do far worse.

But every now and then a teacher would come unstuck. There was a particularly vicious Maths teacher who the kids ganged up on – they went collectively to the Headmistress about him. He was sacked for slapping a few children. I never knew him properly but from what I heard in the staffroom, he was a seriously psychotic character.


## THE LESSONS OF MACBETH

There was one incident that led to my never, ever touching a child again.

I arranged for my form to perform a children's version of *Macbeth* in a whole school assembly. I spent ages preparing it: going through the script and rehearsing with the whole class. On the day of the performance, my lead actor decided that he wasn't going to do the show because he didn't want to re-hearse in the lunch hour and he didn't like the actor who was playing Lady Macbeth. This really irritated me and I said that he was being unreasonable. He had to play Macbeth; we had spent ages practising the play, the whole school was talking about seeing it and even the Headmistress would be in attendance – and she rarely ventured out of her office.

Malik, my Macbeth, shook his head vehemently. The whole class was listening and watching to see who would win this battle. I had never had such resistance from anyone in my form before and felt as though my authority with the class was at stake and my status as a competent teacher was under attack. If the play didn't go ahead, it would look like I had no control over my form, which I had boasted about having such a grip over.

So I decided to do the trusty "grabbing the arm" trick. Malik was a little boy and was sitting at the front of the class. I can still see him now; his snubby little nose was stuck right up in the air and he was shaking his head in the most aggravating manner possible. So I took his arms, lifted him out of his chair and put him back again. "You will be Macbeth, I can assure you of that Malik," I said.

I knew that I had stepped way over the mark as soon as I put Malik down. The class gasped. I had never manhandled any of my form before; only older, more hardened boys who just took such treatment for granted. Malik screamed back at me that he was never going to play Macbeth and that he was going to tell on me.

"I'm going to make a complaint," he shouted as he rushed out of the room as fast as his little legs could carry him.

I tried persisting with the play. I took on the role of Macbeth myself but found that Lady Macbeth, played by Grace, was not delivering her lines but saying, "No, Macbeth, don't shake me, please don't shake me, but you can shake Duncan!"

The class burst out laughing at this point and I called rehearsals to a halt. I asked them to get on with some work as I speculated about my future. Malik went to the Deputy Head, John Priest. At break-time I went down to Priest's office and had a brief discussion with him.

"He's threatening to go to his parents, but we'll sort him out, don't worry," John reassured me. "You're not normally the kind of guy who tonks the kids."

Somehow, John did persuade Malik not to say anything, which was a pretty amazing achievement – Malik seemed determined that the whole world should know about what an ogre I had been.

I was ashamed of myself; I promised to myself that I would never touch a kid again, a promise I have kept.

## MR ALAM

The pernicious consequences of corporal punishment were brought home to me even more vividly when I had to deal with Mr Alam. He approached me for help one blustery afternoon in December. He burst into my room where I was teaching and said, "You must come, you must come..."

I didn't understand the rest. Mr Alam's pronunciation was quite garbled. I had talked to him a little in the staffroom and found him fairly jolly. We would laugh about the total lack of ability of a pupil we both taught, Ikram. Ikram was a kid with special needs; he didn't speak any English although he had been in England for nearly ten years. Mr Alam spoke Bengali and had realised that Ikram's Bengali was very poor as well. "They call him 'thickie' in their dialect," Mr Alam chuckled.

I know this wasn't very charitable but we found it funny. I would have been horrified to be mocking a kid's stupidity a year before but I was beginning to be affected by the school. While I was enjoying it there, it was a very tough place to work; teaching was extremely intensive, there were no days off, every lesson left me feeling drained. This led to a feeling of being punch-drunk and permanently tired. Humour, and black humour in particular, was just about the only weapon there was to combat the sense of depression and futility that could invade those long afternoons.

Mr Alam was a clever man. He had a first-class degree in Physics and ran his own import/export business. He lived in Bromley, in a nice leafy suburb, and sent both his kids to expensive private schools; the combination of the teacher's wage and his business income made him quite a wealthy man. He wore gold jewellery and made it very clear that although he was a Bengali he was of a completely different class to the "peasant children" of Sylhet.

This snobbery and arrogance was at the heart of the problem. He had nothing but contempt for his pupils. They were ignorant scum to him. In India, where he had also taught, he used the cane regularly and beat his charges. They never disobeyed him.

Not so in the East End. That day, as he beckoned me on, I walked into his classroom to find a scene of totally malign pandemonium. I say the word malign because this behaviour was malicious and angry. It made me realise that although I had had kids play up with me it had always been essentially good humoured. Even Hakim's smoking in the classroom had not been a malevolent act; it wasn't an act of hatred towards me.

But everything I saw then made me think that my form hated cheery Mr Alam. They were throwing things at the boards, turning over tables, sweeping bunsen burners off tables, smashing test tubes and fighting each other.

"Scum, scum, they are scum," Alam yelled disconsolately, quite consciously aping a catch-phrase of John Priest. Now this is the interesting thing about language; a word of condemnation sounds completely different in one teacher's mouth from another's. When John Priest said "scum" he really meant "you are normally good kids but now you've really let me down". For all his tough guy, Michael Caine talk, the kids knew that he liked them, that he wanted them to do their best. When Mr Alam said "scum", you could tell that he really meant it.

I shouted for the class to stop and they did for a few moments. I told them that this was not acceptable behaviour but I felt at a loss as to what to do. I had left another difficult class unsupervised down the corridor and wanted to get back to them in case the same thing started happening there.

Alam grabbed Fatih, a naughty tubby boy who had Hassan in an armlock, and yanked him towards me, "This boy. He is very bad. He needs to be punished. He is scum!"

Alam's nostrils were flaring. Fatih had obviously done some pretty disgraceful things. Hassan, who was now released from the armlock, lifted up his head and said, "Mr Alam keeps hitting us, sir. What are we supposed to do?"

I knew Hassan was telling the truth. I could see just from the way that Alam had grabbed Fatih that he was manhandling the kids. In most schools in the country Alam would have been sacked in a minute, but not here. I said that we should get John Priest to come up. Alam shook his head. Suddenly his look changed from one of anger to one of contrition. "No, no, don't do that. You can go now. I'll sort this out."

I didn't know what to say. I turned to leave the room, which seemed a tiny bit calmer. Alam approached me in a confidential manner, "You won't tell anyone about this, will you?"

I didn't reply and left the room.

# PREPARATION FOR AN INSPECTION

When it was announced by the Head that we were going to be inspected by the local authority the following term, I hoped the inspectors would find out about the teachers like Mr Alam who were failing in their duties to teach the kids. I felt powerless myself to do anything about it. All the other teachers knew who the main offenders were but no one made a formal complaint. In many schools with more empowered kids and more attentive parents, these teachers would unquestionably have lost their jobs but at Truss they survived – for the time being.

We were told by the Head of the Local Education Authority in a short speech she gave to staff that the inspection would copy the same procedures as the new Ofsted inspections. "The Truss School has been chosen because we need to investigate how we might raise levels of achievement here," she said. In plain English this really meant the inspectors were going to look at why the results in the school were totally rubbish. For another year running, we were languishing near the bottom of the league tables. However, we weren't bottom this time; that privilege went to Boynton Boys. (What the hell was going on down there? Most of their pupils were white and English-speaking.)

Joe Dicey held a very rare department meeting so that we could prepare for the inspection. It was now February; the inspection would happen during the middle week of March. He gripped the agenda tightly and said, "We are supposed to talk about differentiation. Whatever that is."

Sean and Figgis laughed. Figgis slapped his fist into his palm and said, "Why don't we tell them we're like Millwall: we're rubbish but we're hard!"

More laughter. This time Dicey joined in. The only person who didn't was Brenda Klein; she was an elderly English teacher who, I had been told, had a "history". I wasn't quite sure what this was but I knew that she was Jewish and had relatives who had died in the Holocaust. She was a very bitter woman who hated teaching in the school and couldn't wait to get out; she was regarded as a "nutter" by the rest of the staff because she wouldn't stop complaining. There was nothing she didn't moan about. Top of her list were: the total stupidity of the kids, the appallingness of their behaviour, the subsidence in her house, her terrible insurance company who wouldn't pay up for her house to be fixed, the male chauvinism of the English department and so on.

She taught my form English and I helped support her in a few lessons. She was actually very nice to me. She would lend me novels that she particularly recommended. They were nearly all about disillusioned teachers who hated their jobs. I was quite surprised by how many she was able to produce; they were all hardbacks and out of print.

She clicked her tongue at Figgis's now very familiar Millwall comment. "I suppose this is the sophisticated response that we can expect from this department," she said.

Figgis snarled. He didn't like Brenda. I think her superior learning threatened him. "Well, I haven't seen you do much differentiation!" he said.

Brenda gave one of her trademark high-pitched haughty giggles. "Oh I differentiate with the best of them! If there were prizes for differentiation, I would receive the Nobel! Isn't that so, Francis?"

I nodded doubtfully. I had never seen her differentiate once in all the lessons I had been with her. She taught from the same dog-eared text books she had used twenty years ago. I had a devil of a job trying to explain to the language learners exactly what was going on and had written worksheets galore in order to simplify her tasks for the kids.

Dicey harrumped. "Now that we've covered differentiation, perhaps we should look at the other item: raising achievement. How might we do that?"

"By differentiating?" Sean suggested with a wicked glint in his eye.

Dicey caught his drift immediately and smiled a very rare smile of satisfaction.

"Exactly. And since we seem to have covered that, I think I can officially call this meeting to a close."

With that, Joe and Sean – the Head and Second in Department – cleared out of the room before any of us could say any more.

## THE INSPECTION

Outside the world was going blithely about its business: pigs were snuffling about in the muddy city farm, white vans were crashing over speed bumps, drug dealers were picking up packages in dark alleyways, shopkeepers were reaching for baseball bats to chase away shop-lifting kids.

But inside the school it was different.

Very different.

Inside it was like the invasion of the body-snatchers; there were these people, the inspectors, who looked exactly like teachers in their shabby suits and ill-fitting skirts but weren't. They had been once, but they had gone over to the Other Side. And they knew everything. Absolutely everything. They wanted to invade our bodies and inject their mind-numbing, target-driven, soulless ideology into our veins.

To make matters worse they were stationed in every classroom with their clipboards and detailed charts, scribbling, observing, secretly criticising, down-grading, degrading, nit-picking and, even worse, setting targets. There was no escaping them.

They engendered an atmosphere of panic, recrimi-nation and gloom that I had never seen before. When I entered the staffroom that morning the smokers' corner were all silently sitting at their desks – where they never normally sat – dutifully writing out lesson plans. Not a word was spoken.

But then, just after eight, I found that nearly the whole of the English department had descended upon me in a sudden, gusting storm. Figgis was talk-ing furiously, stamping his feet, Sean Carson was attempting to calm him down, Brenda Klein was chuckling maliciously and Beryl Smith was putting her hand to her forehead and saying, "It's a disaster, it's a total disaster. I can't believe it. We're sunk. It's all going down the plughole and we're all going down with it." Her tone was jocular but edged with doom.

"What's happened?" I asked, still bemused at the sight of Eddie raging so uncontrollably before me. He was virtually crying. "I can't believe it! That bastard! What's he done to us? I had all my lessons planned out, now what am I going to do? *What am I going to do?*"

Sean patted his arm. "Don't worry, dear boy, we'll sort this out. Don't worry."

I had never seen Sean so understanding before. Seeing him trying to comfort Figgis made me realise that he wasn't the ice man that I thought he was. He had feelings too. But even his solace wasn't enough for Figgis. Eddie slumped down in the chair next to the one I was sitting in, flopped his head onto the desk and started to blub. I had never seen a teacher cry like this before and this was quite an unnerving sight. Figgis was weeping like a child. Sean shifted away from him and Pam Drabble approached. She put her arm around Eddie and said that it was all right, everything was going to be all right.

Everyone's sympathy for Figgis surprised me. I suppose I had chalked most people up as quite hard-hearted; the kind who might step over dead bodies if that meant survival. But I was wrong. Very wrong. Sean, Pam, and the other members of smokers' corner were very understanding. Figgis's crying totally changed his relationship with them; he became their pet, their mothered one, after that.

I turned to Beryl and asked her what was going on. She told me in whispered, almost awestruck tones, that Joe Dicey had phoned in sick for two weeks and that he had not deigned to send in his keys. He had the only key to the English Department stock cupboard. All our text books were safely stowed away there.

"Fuck, that means I can't do anything I had been intending to do," I said. However, I wasn't quite up to crying about it. I had to act fast. I left Figgis weeping, as did everyone else, and bolted for my books and then the photocopier[6]. The wait for the blasted machine was

6. The sordid truth about photocopiers: Waiting for the photocopier is probably a teacher's main occupation outside the classroom. Once you finally get on the photocopier, brutal and Machiavellian tactics are employed to get you off it; it starts with little huffings and puffings, then continues with impatient tappings, followed by "How long are you going to be? Do you know I've got a lesson to go to right now?" or "Why are you always on the photocopier? Don't you prepare your lessons properly?" or "The Head has told me that you must stop this right now. This is urgent."

agonising. The school secretary was using it to do a massive batch of bumpf for the inspectors. Eventually, I got on it and, just in the nick of time, was able to run to my form room and register my kids.

In a way I was pleased because I had to do so much rushing around that it took my mind off worrying about what the inspectors might say. Since it was a local authority inspection, Tom Hardy inspected me again, again with the then 10A.

For that year I had a different support teacher with the class. And although I refused to admit it to myself at the time because I liked Colin, having Beryl Smith as ESL support teacher made a massive difference. She did all the things that Colin should have done but didn't. We planned lessons together, she wrote out her own worksheets for the language learners, and, being an experienced English teacher herself, she encouraged me to give the class more challenging material. She helped teach the whole class and keep them in order, she turned up to lessons on time. None of which Colin had done.

Tom Hardy was very impressed by the work he saw the class do. We were doing a unit on advertising. The pupils worked in groups annotating magazine articles looking at the denotations (the visual data) and connotations (the associations created in the reader's mind by the visual data) of the advert. It was a good lesson that was clearly part of a whole series of lessons which would lead to a meaningful piece of work: an essay analysing the techniques used by magazine adverts.

At the end of the lesson, Hardy took me aside and praised the lesson. He then asked whether this was part of the scheme of work suggested by my Head of Department. He didn't refer to Joe by name. I said that it wasn't, that many of the ideas had come from Beryl. Tom Hardy noted this down and went on his way.

I was observed in another lesson. This time things didn't go so well. I was working with Brenda Klein with my form in an English lesson. A portly man I didn't know sidled into the room. We were teaching Charles Lamb's version of *The Tempest* to the children. The language of the Lamb story was difficult and many of the kids were struggling. I had written some multiple choice questions for the kids to do but unfortunately, as happened in most lessons, Brenda wouldn't stop talking.

It was Perky Percy, the Head of ESL, who gave me the feedback for this lesson. Apparently, the inspector was looking at the ESL provision in the school and wasn't impressed by what he saw in Brenda's lesson: inappropriate materials, no variety in teaching techniques, no proper learning objectives, no differentiation and so on. The list was endless.

This report really demotivated me. I felt it was unfair because I had tried to do those things but hadn't had any room for manoeuvre in Brenda's lesson. Having received a positive English report and a negative ESL one, it made me realise that I didn't want to continue being an ESL teacher. I needed to be in charge of things in the classroom.

## THE FINAL REPORT

" I hope they bloody well say that the school is a pit, a pit the like of which Edgar Allen Poe never wrote about. A pit where the pendulum swings and swings above your head and creeps closer and closer until you can feel the very breath of it beside your skin and you know it is going to kill you – but it never does!"

Brenda giggled hysterically as she finished her monologue.[7] She had cornered me in the corridor just outside the meeting room and wouldn't stop giving her pessimistic banter. The staff were waiting to go in and listen to the inspector's final report. It was Judgement Day and Brenda wanted all of us to be damned. This wasn't the general wish of most of the staff but there were a few, a desperately disillusioned few, who delighted in the thought that the whole shithouse might go up in flames.

Eventually we were ushered in and the staff sat tensely on the cushioned seats of the plush meeting room – which was normally out of bounds – to await the verdict. The Chief Inspector came in and announced that overall Truss was judged to be satisfactory with some serious weaknesses. Apart from Brenda and a couple of doom-mongers, there was a big sigh of relief at this because if the school had been judged unsatisfactory there was a possibility that it might have to be closed down.[8] This was what the government was threatening to do with failing schools. The adjective "satisfactory" meant that all of our jobs were safe. The Chief Inspector went on to say that

---

7. Obsessive Compulsive Talking Disorder: There are always a few in every school who suffer from this lamentable condition. These are teachers who talk endlessly at their classes, never listen to anything anyone says, and then do exactly the same with other members of staff.

pupil discipline was generally good in the school. Now you might find that surprising to hear, but the fact is that many of the inspectors had seen far worse behaviour in inner-city schools and that in most lessons most of the pupils were reasonably well behaved. She said that most of the English, drama, PE, geography and history lessons were judged to be satisfactory.

However, it was felt that there were some serious weaknesses in the geography lessons and that the management of the English and ESL departments needed attention. It also commented that the school needed to lose a Deputy Head because it had three: John Priest, who was in charge of the Upper School, Henry Williams who supervised the Lower School, and the Headmistress's pal, Wendy Jones, who oversaw the curriculum.

8. Teacher-school co-dependency You may wonder why the staff didn't cheer at the thought of the source of their misery being closed down, but that would be to misunderstand the nature of many teachers' relationships with schools.

Teachers become very attached to their institutional pain; its ghastliness is their main topic of conversation, its meagre wage is their means of living, its timetable the structure of their lives. It is the hateful drug which is simultaneously destroying and sustaining them.

# INSPECTION FALLOUT

The Headmistress was slow to react to the report. No one was asked to leave, no one was sacked. The school carried on exactly as before but things were different.

Joe, for one thing, didn't return to school for quite a while and when he did, he kept taking days off. He wanted out but he wasn't going to go without negotiating a good retirement package; retiring on grounds of ill health was apparently much more lucrative than not. So the English department lurched on into summer not quite knowing what was going to happen to its leader.

Meanwhile major things were happening in the ESL department. It was rebranded the "English As An Additional Language" department, the "EAL" department, and the Home Office gave it a large injection of cash.

It was decided that a second in department would be appointed, together with a resources manager, and a home liaison officer. Because I had decided that I wanted to get a full-time English post, I held back from applying for any of the posts. The home liaison officer position went to a young, pleasant Bengali-speaking teacher, the resources manager to a more elderly one and second in department was given to Colin.

There had only been two people in major contention for the second in department job: Colin and Beryl Smith. Beryl was obviously, in my view, a far better candidate: she worked hard, she knew a lot, she was good with all the theory. But she was new to the school, a middle-aged woman who had a tendency to "natter" too much and she was primarily an English teacher.

Colin, on the other hand, had been at the school for seven years, had poise and discretion, got on with most of the staff and had been teaching ESL for a long time.

"It's jobs for the boys," Beryl said to me with only the barest trace of bitterness. "Colin won't do anything but he and Percy will chunter away, making all the right noises and they'll pretend to the Head that they are doing great things. But we'll know it will be a sham. Besides, I have a funny feeling about Colin. I think there is something not right there."

All of her predictions were proven to be right. Some more than she could have possibly known.

# A WEEK IN THE COUNTRY

During the summer term, I took my form, 7Q, to the school's rural studies centre in Wales. Because it was part of an age-old foundation that owned a lot of property, the school actually had its very own rural studies centre situated in the gorgeous Welsh hills. Unfortunately, the foundation had decided that it couldn't afford to maintain the centre and that it would have to close at the end of the year.

Quite a few of the kids didn't want to go. They were frightened of what might happen in Wales. Rumours had been spread that ghastly things happened there. At the time, we just put this down to superstitions and overactive imaginations. I was commissioned by Sharon Day to visit the homes of the refusers and persuade them to come along.

This time I went alone. I visited a series of bleak flats where there were no carpets, no proper furniture, and mothers who didn't speak much English. The kids loved the fact that I was visiting their homes. They jumped up and down and shouted that Mr Gilbert had come to see them. In all cases except one, I was able to persuade the parents to let their children go.

Then on one bright May morning, I left school

at dawn with my form, navigated the Tube with them and reached Paddington. It was bedlam as I shepherded them onto the train. A teacher from the studies centre, Alice, met me on the platform and together we managed to find our seats. The train journey was a long one and the children were very raucous. A lonely and disturbed boy in the form, Bashir Rahman, got into two fights and ended up getting hit on the head by Hassan – who was wearing a nasty fat ring that cut and bruised Bashir's face.

The first thing I knew about it all was that Bashir was suddenly standing on his seat and pummelling Hassan Miah with his fists. I calmly asked Bashir to go to the back of the carriage, away from the other kids. Hassan was badly stunned and hurt, practically crying from the shame of having such a puny, skinny kid like Bashir make mincemeat of him. As I took Bashir to the back of the train, he swore, "Fucking cunts. Cunt boys. Cunt boys."

I rubbed my forehead, wondering what we were supposed to do with a boy like Bashir. He lived with his mother and seemed to be always moving around; he'd come late into the school and seemed to have no fixed abode. He spoke very little English, couldn't read or write, had no friends, virtually no home, he was as small as an eight-year-old and as angry as a suicidal teenager.

The white passengers sitting next to us clearly felt threatened by so many brown faces and a few of them complained to us about the noise. I tried to quieten the kids down but without much success. They were far too excited. This was the first time some of them had ever left London. Certainly, it was the first time any of them had been to Wales.

\*\*\*

The studies centre was situated in a breathtakingly beautiful place near Prestatyn in north Wales. The kids fell in love with it immediately. They ran across the crystal-clear streams which babbled over mossy rocks and slates, they played hide-and-seek amidst the oak trees, they scuttled around the eery, wooden corridors of the converted farmhouse and chucked stones down the slope which revealed a tapering vista of mountains and valleys.

For the first time ever, I felt totally liberated with the kids. I could be myself and not worry. I dropped all pretence of being a teacher, stopped shushing them and telling them off because there appeared to be no need.

Outside, the kids could shriek and rush around as much as they wanted and it didn't make the blindest bit of difference. I played tag with them, potted billiard balls and knocked around a ping-pong ball in the games room, positioned myself on the wing in a football match and went with them on nightly excursions into the woods.

The centre was brilliantly resourced. There was an amazing open-plan classroom with an aquarium and a lot of scientific equipment. In the garden there was a stile and a long rope ladder which allowed exciting access to a flourishing meadow. There was a chicken coop, a herd of goats, an adventure playground built out of branches and nets where no kid was allowed to touch the ground.

The people who ran the studies centre were originally teachers at Truss but had leapt at the opportunity to run the centre when it opened twenty-five years ago. Now their whole lives were based in Wales and they had no intention of leaving when the centre closed at the end of the year.

"The Headmistress has offered me a job teaching geography at the school if I want it," said Clive, the head of the centre. "But I wouldn't take it even if they gave me a million pounds. It's too much like crowd control there. I would prefer to be unemployed here than go back there."

This kind of talk really depressed me. Although Clive was a good teacher, he simply didn't feel that there was an opportunity to do good teaching at Truss.

\*\*\*

The change that occurred in the kids over the week was remarkable. Clive and his team kept them very busy: every morning they would hike into the hills and collect specimens to bring back and analyse in the laboratory at the centre. They would go bird-watching, learn about the different trees in the forest, investigate the geology of the area. Once they had completed their work by the early afternoon, they were free to play in the neighbouring fields and woods.

In the evening everyone would have to help make the evening meal, do chores and then, after supper, play the board and card games in the library or read.

\*\*\*

Grace was locked in her room all night for allowing the showers to flood; it had been her duty to look after them. She screamed for a little bit that there was a green-eyed monster at her window; when Alice and I went into the room, we found out that it was an inquisitive owl poking his nose at the glass. After that tempestuous night, Grace improved a great deal and was given the overall responsibility of keeping the kitchen clean. Although she was rather too bossy at certain times, I was amazed at how seriously she took her duties. She drew up a timetable for everyone and would make sure that it was enforced.

Shahana likewise enjoyed being in charge of the wellington boots (of which the centre had a great many) and raincoats.

Hassan and Fatih, the two hard men of the form, were not so good at fulfilling their responsibilities but greatly enjoyed playing hide-and-seek with me and a few others in the woods. However, Clive did make sure that they did their bit; they served out the dinner on a couple of nights.

On one day we drove along winding roads to the source of the river Enion, which was basically a bog on a hill. We followed the thickening stream downhill through some very treacherous marshy terrain. The pine-wood forest that enfolded the stream was difficult to navigate and the slimy rocks at the edge of the water succeeded in making the boys very wet very quickly. They loved it.

Bashir proved himself to be a surprisingly good climber until he fell into the stream. Instead of crying hysterically, I was surprised to see that he was laughing. It was amazing! I had never seen Bashir laugh before.

That night we walked up Foel Fawr – a big, bald hill – and Bashir, having been taught the word by Clive, shouted "Geronimo!" He rushed down the hill at great speed and seeing that he had come to a precipice, instead of stopping, opened his arms like a bird and tried to fly, but fell flat on the road. It was a miracle that nothing was broken. He only grazed his hand. Again, there was more laughter.

It was a poignant image watching Bashir trying to fly. I can still see it all these years later.

\*\*\*

On Wednesday night, the children went camping with Clive and Alice in the wilds of the woods, leaving me by myself in the spooky farmhouse. They returned the next morning with tales of darkness and bugs and extreme cold.

Clive was clearly exhausted with having to deal with them all night. Over coffee that morning, he repeated a familiar mantra, "Teaching at Truss isn't teaching at all; it's more like child-minding. I'd get out if I were you. Get out before it's too late. There are a lot of teachers who have got stuck at Truss. You don't want that to happen to you, do you? Being there more than a few years makes you unemployable anywhere else because the better schools that you might want to go to think you've just been child-minding. They think you haven't actually taught a proper lesson for the whole time you've been there. Now, that is probably a tad harsh but it is what a lot of them think. A lot of teachers get stuck at Truss. A lot."

I didn't reply but secretly thought that maybe he had a point. Later that day, I realised that Bashir only had one pair of clothes. He slept in his day clothes – even if they were wet.

This realisation made me sad. He had nothing; he had no proper home, no friends, no self-esteem and no money. And yet, being only a few days in the country had changed him; he'd learnt to skim stones across the stream, he'd started joining in with football and he'd acquired – thanks to Clive – a whole new set of clothes.

I could see that Clive's dismissal of the kids was just an act. He cared about them deeply; his constant encouragement of Bashir showed me that. He spent a lot of time with him during the week when he really would have been much better off not to; Bashir was uncommunicative and aggressive quite a bit of the time. But Clive won through.

There were tears in Bashir's eyes as he waved good-bye to Clive on the final day. Were those the happiest days of Bashir's life? I am fairly certain they were.

## BACK TO LONDON

"Will you be quiet? I need you to be quiet. I'm waiting. *I'm waiting*. Will you listen to what I am saying? Is anyone listening? Fatih, you're not listening. Grace, you're not listening. Bashir, stop fighting. No, Hassan, don't punch Fatih. Will you be quiet? I am asking you to be quiet. I AM TELLING YOU ALL TO SHUT UP! SHUT UP!"

My blood pressure has sky-rocketed. I can feel the blood bubbling against my cheeks. My head is throbbing from the noise and humiliation of it all and still the class is not listening. It is the beginning of the new academic year and everything has changed. My mind is constantly comparing the form with last year; they would listen to me immediately last year, I had rarely had to shout and never lost my temper. But now, look at them! They are so busy jabbering away amongst themselves that they scarcely have time to listen to their teacher. Somewhat ironically, I feel the rural studies centre is to blame. In Wales, the environment of the study centre had enabled me to be much freer with the kids. I didn't have to worry obsessively about whether they were behaving themselves; there were space and air and things to do there.

Back in the cramped classroom the extra latitude I gave to the pupils in my form rebounds back on me; they are so much more confident, so much more enthusiastic, so much more difficult to handle. Before, I had kept their genies firmly corked up in their bottles but now they are all flitting crazily around the room.

## STARING AT THE *TES*

It was in that bleak first week back, the beginning of my third year back at Truss, that I began to look at the *Times Educational Supplement* in a very different way. It changed from being a rather boring rag full of tedious news about moaning, groaning teachers to being a possible passport out of the depression that was beginning to engulf me.

I bought it on Friday, tossed away the news section immediately and scrambled to look at the jobs. I scanned all the English jobs in London and began to fantasize about teaching in places like Bromley, Waltham Forest, Redbridge, Havering... the outskirts of the city, away from the poverty, away from the noise and the incessant fill-in-the-gaps sheets. I looked at the jobs on offer and dreamed of large classrooms with docile kids who could be relied upon to bring their books to the lessons, to do their homework, who had reading ages above that of seven-year-olds. These places shimmered in the distant horizons of my mind as gleaming bastions of enlightenment and learning.

The next week, I surreptitiously sneaked out of school at lunchtime and phoned up a few schools offering full-time English jobs and asked the secretaries there to send me their details and application forms. They soon started flooding through my postbox. My evenings from this time onward were spent filling them in.

But I hadn't told anyone in the school that this was what I was doing – except the Headmistress who had been predictably sniffy about it. "You know Brenda will be retiring soon and there should be an opening here for a full-time English post," she said. "I can't see why we are any worse than anywhere else. And as for your desire to teach A-Level English, well, I have taught A-Level and I can tell you that it is no more rewarding than teaching Year 7."

However, she did agree to write me a reference.

## THE YELLOW SERE

"Your form are getting on so well. They're fab – absolutely fabulous," said Sharon Day. "They seem so much happier since they got back from Wales. You've done a great job with them."

She leaned towards me and patted my arm. We were nearly six weeks into term and I hadn't received a single interview after applying for about ten jobs. Not one bloody interview. What was wrong with me? Why was my form not listening to a word I was saying? Was I a rubbish teacher? Was there something fundamentally wrong with me? I bowed my head and swallowed hard. I was beginning to feel very, very sorry for myself.

"There isn't anything the matter, is there, Francis?" Sharon asked.

"No, no, I'm fine," I said. The last thing I wanted to do was to admit to Sharon that I was having real difficulties with my form when it appeared that no one else was. And I certainly didn't want to tell her that I had applied for a trillion jobs because I was desperate to get away.

I left her office feeling like tears were only one serious incident away. I joined my Year 10 English form where I found Colin sitting at the back of the class chatting with Wahid. Both of them laughed as I entered. I blinked. What was going on over there? Colin was leaning back in his chair in much the same way as Wahid and appeared to be sneering at me.

I tensed up. This was the last thing I needed right now; my support teacher was openly mocking me in front of the kids. I controlled myself and asked if there was a problem.

"We were just saying that you look like your life has fallen into the yellow sere," Colin quipped merrily.

"You gotta that yellow sere look!" Wahid added, flicking his hands in the way that tough boys did.

We were studying the last act of *Macbeth* in class so it was just possible that Wahid knew what Colin was talking about, but I doubted it.

I asked to speak to Colin outside the classroom. I didn't like being called a withered depressive, albeit in Shakespearean language.

Colin denied my request by saying, "Don't you think you should start with the lesson? You were late anyway and we do have the last act of *Macbeth* to read."

About half of the class – the half that understood English – laughed and the others were soon joining in. This was intolerable. Not only did I have a difficult class to contend with but it seemed that most of the disruption was caused by a teacher. Somehow I found the energy to press on with the lesson. I had all my fill-in-the-blank sheets ready to go. Despite my poor morale, my instinct for survival was making me prepare for my lessons every night.

The lesson progressed in its average ghastly fashion with Wahid and Yumni spending most of the time wandering around the class trying to steal other people's rubbers, Bilal making snide remarks about how ill I looked, the others intermittently inserting misspelt words in the gaps, and Colin talking in chuckling monosyllables with Ikram and doing doodles of Macbeth staring at walking trees.

I walked away from the lesson in disgust when the bell went but then, halfway down the corridor, decided to go back and tackle Colin. He was still sitting in the classroom with Ikram completing his doodle of Dunsinane castle. He smiled with sickening graciousness at me.

"Yes, Mr Gilbert, how can I help you?" he said.

The others had left and I knew that Ikram wouldn't understand anything we said, so I spoke my mind.

"That was totally out of order," I said. "You were encouraging those kids to laugh at me!"

Colin chuckled and shook his head.

"Just relax, Francis! They like you. You're too uptight. You should see the funny side."

I had been prepared to really lose it with him but his saying, "They like you" totally wrong-footed me. He was saying that I was a popular teacher. He was saying that I had won their affection. Suddenly, I found myself backtracking.

"Look, maybe I took it the wrong way. Sorry, I just, I just..." I faltered and then left the room.

# TABOO TALK

I wanted to talk to Figgis about Colin, but it was difficult. There was an unwritten rule that there were certain teachers that were never discussed. There were a few who were fair game and could be endlessly slagged off – the Head, her mate Wendy, a couple of Year Heads, Joe Dicey and Perky Percy – but there were quite a few who were definitely out of bounds. Sean headed this list, but Colin wasn't far behind. He was someone who was beyond reproach; anything he did wrong was because he was a victim of someone else's machinations.

But finally I plucked up enough courage during one lunch hour when Figgis was clearing up his classroom and the October rain was lashing the playground outside, and said, "How do you find Colin? How is he in your lessons – he supports you, doesn't he?"

Figgis looked at me quizzically. He knew that I had crossed an unspoken boundary. He thought for a moment and then said, "He's absolutely fucking useless. Totally useless."

I breathed a big sigh of relief. It wasn't just me!

"But why does no one say anything? Why did he get promoted to being Second in Department?"

Figgis smiled ruefully. "Oh come on, Francis, you should have worked that one out by now. Do you think getting promoted in teaching is anything to do with talent? I mean, if that was the case, you and me would be running the school by now. We're the only people who have any brains in this place, but that isn't how it works. You get promoted because you are not a threat. Colin makes Perky Percy look good. Percy is incompetent and Colin is incompetent and lazy."

I suspected that Figgis was telling the truth – and I felt quite flattered by his comments – but I was still puzzled.

"But why does no one say anything about him? Why aren't we allowed to moan about him?"

"Everyone feels sorry for him. They pity him. Apparently, he had a really bad childhood and his girlfriend left him and he lives in Norfolk and has to drive four hours every day. He's a sad character really," Figgis said.

\*\*\*

Gloom descended upon me. I had always thought of Colin as an essentially transcendent character, someone who maintained his jolly cheerfulness despite the fact that he was surrounded by misery on all sides: the miserable social conditions of the kids, the miserable working conditions of being a teacher and so on. But I could see now Figgis was right. Colin's merriness was all an act. His chuckling joviality was a mask for deep unhappiness and unease.

He was yet another person trapped at Truss. And I didn't want to think about this, so I told Figgis that I had some preparation to do and left his classroom. As I walked down the corridor, I began to feel like a heavy weight was pressing down on my head; images of Wahid and Colin and the rest of 10A laughing at me danced before my eyes, my red, red eyes. Was that my fate for the rest of my life?

The weight grew heavier and heavier. I was beginning to feel a terrible headache coming on. I felt as though I was about to suffocate. I had three more one-hour-and-fifteen-minute lessons to teach and then there were still Wednesday, Thursday and Friday to go. Jesus Christ, how was I going to get through the rest of the week feeling like this? I had to get some air, get away from the smelly socks, away from the smoky, fuggy staffroom, away from the ear-splitting noise of the classrooms...

I staggered along the corridor and found myself

outside the Headmistress's office. Suddenly, I was gripped with a desire to know whether any of the schools I had applied to had asked for a reference; this, at least, would be some indication that they were interested. I pushed into her secretary's office and found Joan sitting at her computer.

"Are you OK?" Joan asked sympathetically. "You look really ill."

I slumped into the chair next to her desk.

"I was just wondering whether any school had asked for a reference. I've been applying for other jobs," I said glumly.

"Very wise," Joan said. "But, no, unfortunately, there have been no requests. No luck this time."

I got up to go. I didn't know what else to say but I would have liked to have stayed. Joan was clearly sympathetic to my plight. Just as I was leaving, she said, "You do know how to fill in those application forms, don't you? You do know that when the schools write out a job specification you must answer each one fully; then, by law, they have to give you an interview. That's the new world of equal opportunities."

I wasn't quite sure what Joan was talking about, so I walked back into the room. Joan got out some job application packs that Truss had drawn up and showed me that applying for a job was a precise, bureaucratic exercise; it was a question of speaking the lingo of each individual school. I hadn't understood this before and had just been writing more or less the same thing in every supporting statement I had written.

"So that's why you're not getting anywhere! You've got to start answering the job spec, my boy!" Joan said. "We'll see you safely out of here yet. You're very wise, you know. I've just seen the forecasts for next year's budget – we've got to make some quite hefty savings in ESL. There are going to be redundancies, I'm afraid."

## MAGICAL MISSIVES

Joan's advice lifted my spirits and I applied for the next two English jobs with renewed vigour, answering the job specs in full. And miracle of miracles, I got two interviews! The only catch was that they were on the same day and one of them was at a school, Wickstead, where I had been an unhappy pupil for a term when I was eleven years old.

But by this time I had worked myself up into such a state that anywhere would have been preferable to

Truss. This was quite unfair on the school and more reflective of my psychological state at the time but it might help explain what happened next.

You cannot conceive of the happiness I felt at seeing those two letters on official notepaper inviting me for interview. I slipped them into my jacket pocket and carried them around with me like lucky charms while I was teaching. I had not one, but two interviews! After months of failure, finally there was some sort of light speckling the walls of my tunnel; the scent of fresh air was permeating the darkness.

The grand interview day was the second from last day of the half-term. This meant that if I failed to get the jobs I would be more or less compelled to stay at Truss until April at the very earliest because of the regulations about resignations. However, if I got a job, I would hand in my notice on the Friday, teach until Christmas and be starting my new job in January. Knowing this ratcheted up the pressure even more because I wanted out pretty damn fast.

I phoned both of my possible new places of employment and found out that the interviews were scheduled at exactly the same times. The schools were a considerable distance from each other: one in Barnet, one in Redbridge. I thought for one ghastly moment that I would have to withdraw from one, but then the obliging headmistress at the Barnet school helped me work out a plan: I could look round her school in the morning, get a taxi to Wickstead, the Redbridge school, for lunch, complete my interview at Wickstead and then be interviewed in Barnet at about 4pm. It was a tight schedule but I was up for it. It smelt of freedom!

## JUDGEMENT DAY

I couldn't sleep the night before the Massively Important Day. I was unbearable; I phoned an older friend of mine who was a Head of English and grilled her for about an hour on what the panel would be looking for in the interview, I practised my answers over and over again with my wife, I laid out my new suit (specially bought for the occasion) and checked and double-checked all the equipment I needed. I was more prepared than a meal at a five-star French restaurant.

I leapt out of bed on the fateful morning and gathered all my stuff together, leaving in plenty of time so that I would arrive early and check out the surrounding area of the Barnet school before being given the guided tour. I had been advised by Perky Percy to examine how the pupils entered the school; whether they were in uniform, whether they were behaving, whether they seemed happy and so on.

Unfortunately, when I got to the tube station I realised that I had forgotten to wear my glasses. Normally, I put them on first thing in the morning because my eyesight is not that great but in my excitement I had forgotten to do this and hadn't even noticed that all the trees and cars in the street were rather blurred. It wasn't until I saw the smudgy lights of an oncoming tube train that I realised.

This caused me to fly into a great panic. I rushed up the escalator, out of the station, along the streets and back to our flat where I found – oh catastrophe! – that my glasses were no longer there and neither was my wife. Where were they? Hell, now I wouldn't even be able to see my interviewers. I would be squinting all day. I would look like a complete weirdo and there was no way I could admit to forgetting my glasses; I would look like a disorganised pranny!

I wrote a furious note: WHERE THE HELL ARE MY GLASSES?! and then departed in a foul temper back to the tube station, groping my way along the street and cursing the world and my wife for my incredible vanishing spectacles. Perhaps I was doomed. Perhaps the Truss Book Of Fate had decreed I was doomed to stay there, or even worse, face the humiliation of being sacked from a school like Truss.

I took the Northern line to Barnet and found out that I was just in the nick of time for my guided tour. It was a top-achieving girls' school and seemed like paradise to me; beautiful displays were mounted in the corridors, the girls wandered around sedately and without shouting. And the teachers looked remarkably unstressed. The Headmistress was in her early forties and quite eccentric. She gave me the guided tour, showing me immaculate classrooms, girls working in silence in English, superbly resourced laboratories and spacious, leafy recreational grounds.

My mouth was wide-open. Even the minor public school I had gone to wasn't as nice as this; everything was purpose-built and wonderfully well maintained. And this was a state school. No wonder they had a thousand applicants for a hundred places.

"We can pick the cream here," the Headmistress purred. "There are never any discipline problems. If you got the job, you would really be able to teach to the highest level. But are you up to it?"

Despite her haughty words and manner, I sensed

that she wasn't being patronising. She was secure enough in herself not to lord it over me. She was genuinely concerned about whether, having been at such an inner-city school, I would be able to cope with the marking load, the lesson preparation. I explained my academic qualifications to her and she seemed impressed. I realised that, despite the fact that there would be a formal interview later on in the day, this informal little chat over coffee in her office was the real interview. She was able to ask the real questions that needed asking, not the bureaucratic stuff about differentiation and equal opps and so on which they were required to ask.

Eventually, she lit a cigarette and said in a low whisper, "Look, I like you, Francis. I think you would be good at this school. But I know you've got another interview, so you go away and try your best for that. What kind of school is that?"

I explained that it was a mixed-sex comprehensive which was relatively good. She sucked on her cigarette and reflected. "You'll get that job. You're good. I can see that you're potential headship material. You've done your stint in a tough inner-city comp and now you're spreading your wings which is very good. But I have to tell you, there is an internal candidate going for this job. And she's a woman. You know what I mean?"

She winked at me. She seemed to be sending me some very mixed signals; on the one hand, she clearly liked me and had said some stuff which had sent my confidence soaring, but, on the other hand, she was saying something else. What did she mean by an internal candidate?[9]

Just at that moment, her phone rang and she picked it up. She frowned and then smiled as she listened to the earpiece. She put down the receiver and said, "It appears that your wife is downstairs at reception where she has your glasses!"

I froze. Oh my God, this was terrible. I was looking like a total idiot.

"What an excellent woman!" the Headmistress continued. "Apparently, she's come all the way from central London to deliver them to you. My oh my, you are lucky to have such a partner!"

Erica, I suppose trying to be tactful, had disappeared by the time I got down to reception where I

---

9.Internal candidates: This is usually a euphemism for a "stitch-up". Schools are obliged by law to interview for posts but if they have a student teacher at the school or someone on a temporary contract who is remotely competent they will plump for him or her, because they've seen them operate for a long time in and out of the classroom.

found my glasses waiting for me. I strapped them over my face and ordered my cab to Wickstead. The driver arrived quickly and together we whisked through the north London traffic towards the eastern suburbs. A few years ago, I would have hated to be going back to the places where I grew up – I had had quite a miserable time there – but now I was very grateful to see so many familiar sites: the old Victorian houses, the well-tended green, the cake-and-bun shops, the civilised library and the clean, tree-lined pavements.

*\*\**

It was very weird walking into the school. The smells of the dining hall – the canteen custard and chip smells mingled with the polished smell of the wooden floor and wainscotting – immediately transported me back to when I was eleven. I had a vision of myself crying as I left the school for the last time. My parents wanted me to go to the local public school but, although they had tried to persuade me that this was what I wanted to do, I remembered now that this wasn't the case. I had friends at Wickstead. Good friends. Martin and Barry and David. And I had cried as I waved goodbye to them.

I never really saw them again. God, why had I just dropped them? Did I learn to be ashamed of Wickstead as I wandered around the quadrangles and old mullioned corridors of my new school?

But now I was back and Martin and Barry and David were grown men and so was I. I had an interview to do. My memories of the school fortified me because as I strolled down the corridors and saw where I used to have English and Maths and recalled the teachers I had had, I began to realise that I had remembered the school incorrectly. My buried, subconscious memories of the school were warm and friendly. I had been wrong thinking for all these years that my time at Wickstead had been miserable.

I began to brighten up as this realisation dawned upon me. Yes, I had a good feeling about this institution; I felt as though I knew it intimately. The school secretaries were friendly and escorted me to the English department where I met, much to my surprise, George Cross whom I remembered very vividly. He was a small, bustling garrulous man who looked rather like Mr Pinkwhistle. He explained in somewhat exasperated tones that they had recruited a probationary teacher who had put up a few posters of Bob Dylan and Morrissey in his classroom on the first day and then phoned in sick for the rest of the term. Apparently, they'd hired a drug addict and he needed to go to a clinic to dry out.

"So you'll be taking over his timetable," George explained and showed it to me.

I was overjoyed when I saw it. Nearly half my timetable was A-Level English Literature and Language – two subjects I was desperate to teach – and the rest was lower school, including GCSE, English. The department's results were phenomenal: 100 per cent pass rate for the old English coursework GCSE – where the entire subject was examined by coursework. George then introduced me to an attractive blonde English teacher who would be teaching next door to me.

I would have my very own classroom – something only the really experienced teachers had at Truss – and it was large, neat and tidy and overlooked lovingly tended gardens and trees.

I punched my hand in delight. This was the place for me. I felt as though, by teaching there, I could reclaim all that friendliness that I had lost in my childhood. I could sense already that it was a happy and secure place which was not riven by terrible social problems and yet took a wide cross-section of kids from all types of backgrounds. It was a genuine comprehensive.

\*\*\*

I decided not to tell anyone in my interview that I had been a pupil at the school for a term because I thought it might prejudice my chances if they knew I had left the school in the way I had. Instead I told the young head teacher and his deputy about how I had taught *Macbeth* and sophisticated literary concepts to the pupils at Truss. They seemed impressed by my efforts and seemed to be pleased with my comments about how to control difficult classes. They appeared to like my enthusiasm for the school and smiled as they listened to me enthuse about my possible timetable.

"I would really love to teach at a more intellectual level now. I've seen the timetable I would take over and I think it looks like heaven!" I said, trying not to let my desperation for the job get the better of me.

"So if I offered you the job would you take it?" the head teacher asked.

"Most definitely," I said.

The head teacher nodded and said that he had two other candidates to interview and would be in touch very shortly. I explained about the other interview I had to go to in Barnet and he said that I should phone him at 3.30pm when he should have made a decision.

Immediately after the interview, I dived into another taxi and went back up to Barnet. My heart was thumping very wildly. I felt as though the interview had gone well but I still wasn't sure whether they would take me because I didn't have that much experience teaching mainstream English.

However, I was in high spirits when I entered the girls' school again. Looking at the school, I realised that it wouldn't be as challenging as Wickstead; it was a much more polite and restrained place. Also, when I met the Head of English it became clear to me that she and her deputy were hogging all the A-Level teaching; I would only teach lower-school classes because, as the lady-like Head of English said, "We need to see how good you are before we can trust you with A-Level. We take it very seriously here."

All the other candidates I met at the "seminar" with the Head of English were women and frightfully well-spoken. I knew that I wouldn't enjoy the school as much as Wickstead but I would take the job if they offered it to me.

My interview was scheduled for four o'clock so I was able to call Wickstead from the staffroom before going in front of the dignitaries of the school. My hands were sweating as I picked up the receiver and dialled. It took a while for the secretary to get the head teacher. By this time I was shaking.

"Mr Gilbert, we're very pleased to offer you the job," he said. "We would be delighted if you joined us in January and we've even decided to give you some extra money if you'll be an English teacher here. Do you accept?"

It is quite sad to say that this was one of the best moments of my life up until then. Of course, there are all those more personal moments like partying the night away, kissing your heart's desire, getting married – those are fantastic – but nothing, in my book, quite compares with the feeling of escape. Wow! I was going to be cruising out of Truss very shortly, away from urban deprivation and ear-splitting classes and fill-in-the-gap sheets and cruising into my very own pretty, big classroom and responsive, quiet students and intellectual challenges. I was headed for paradise and nothing could stop me.

"Yes, I accept, I accept," I said, with tears edging out of my eyes.

"Brilliant! And you'll withdraw from your current interview?"

"Of course," I said.

When I put down the phone, the demure denizens of the staffroom seemed quite shocked to see me dancing around the coffee counter and shouting out, "I did it! I did it!" Just at that moment, the Headmistress entered and said that it was time for my interview. I calmed down and explained that I had been offered the job. She smiled and said that I might as well do the interview anyway.

I breezed into her study and sat down before a panel of middle-aged, buttoned-up women. I should have been nervous but I wasn't; I shone with confidence and answered every question they fired at me – and they were tough questions – with total ease. I was then told to wait in the staffroom. I realised now that this was all a formality because I had no intention of taking the job and they had no intention of offering it to me. It was a foregone conclusion; they had picked their person before the interview day.

And sure enough, a few minutes after my interview, the internal candidate was called into the Headmistress's office. The first one called to the Head's office *always* gets the job.

# DEMOB HAPPY

The window swung open on the second floor and Sean poked his head out of his classroom. "So did you make it?" he asked.

It was seven-thirty the morning after my interview day, the last day of the first half-term.

"I made it," I said with a big grin.

Inside the staffroom I was greeted by the majority of smokers' corner who made the trip around the partition to congratulate me. The women kissed me on the cheeks and John Priest shook my hand while still puffing on his cigar. Their warmth towards me was surprising; all of them genuinely wished me well. There wasn't a trace of envy or resentment in their smiling, careworn faces.

However, there was no sign of Colin. I asked after him.

"We're very worried about him," Pam said. "He had a car accident yesterday. He's fine but he could have killed himself. He went through the barrier on the motorway at five in the morning. His car is a write-off. It's all quite bad. And to make matters worse, I went to his form group to ask them to sign a get-well card and none of them would do it. Dean even said that he deserved it! I gave him a right bollocking!"

I frowned. I left the smokers' corner puzzling over this conundrum as I mounted the stairs and headed for Sharon Day's office. I passed Figgis on the way. He gave me a high five when I told him my news and then said, "But you do realise that you won't be able to say that you're hard any more, don't you?"

"I know, I know," I admitted.

Sharon Day kissed me profusely and congratulated me heartily and then said what I was dreading, "But Francis, what about your form? How are they going to cope without you? What are they going to do? What are we going to tell them?"

These comments needled me – because I knew she was right. I had built up a relationship with nearly every kid in the group and that was going to be severed. All that hard work was going to be for nothing. Or was it? Sharon and I agreed that we would tell them about my leaving straightaway so that we would get used to the idea; they had eight weeks to adjust to my going.

Seeing Joan in the Head's office provided a suitable tonic. "You did the right thing. I don't think this show is going to be on the road for much longer," she said, pointing at the Head's door and then leaning more closely towards me whispered, "The governors are trying to get rid of her."

With that she handed me the necessary paperwork for handing in my resignation. I completed it then and there, because today was the last day I could resign in order to start a new job in January if I wanted to be paid over the Christmas holidays.

\*\*\*

The last eight weeks at Truss were not difficult. Nothing was scary anymore. This made me realise that actually there was nothing endemically wrong with my classes; it was my attitude that was at fault. Once I had a bit of energy and hope, I found that teaching everyone was enjoyable! I found the pupils' tricks and jokes, their squabbles and idiosyncrasies interesting and revealing. It was as though there was a protective shield around me; I was insulated by optimism. Their cusses and disruptions appeared at one remove from me; I could see that the trouble they caused was not my fault, that I was not personally accountable for everything they did in the classroom, and that I could keep them at a distance while trying to teach them.

I only saw Colin intermittently during the term. His attendance became increasingly erratic and when he did turn up he was more inclined to sit at the back of the class and share hushed jokes with Wahid than try to assist the ESL learners. He had even dropped the semblance of trying to help. Because I was leaving and because I didn't want to cause a fuss, I never properly complained other than talking to Figgis about it.

## DEPARTURE

My form held a "surprise" party on the last day of term which Pam had helped to arrange. There was orangeade and crisps and little chocolate bars and music. Quite a few of the pupils were still rueful about my departure and kept asking me if I would change my mind about leaving.

"What about Wales? Who have we got to go to Wales with now?" Hassan said.

"And who can teach us *Macbeth*?" Grace chirped cheekily, recalling my disastrous attempts at trying to put on the play.

"And who will look after us in the mornings?" Suraya said. She was a girl who liked the fact that I was always in the form room at eight o'clock and ready to help her with her homework and reading.

Other pupils, like Fatih and Bashir, who I had had major dealings with over work and behaviour, sulked in the background not saying anything. I knew that if I thought too much about it all I would feel over-whelmed by sadness and so I decided to distract myself with the festivities.

*\*\**

The leaving presentation given by the Headmistress was more muted and less celebratory. Joe Dicey and several other long-term staff were leaving on the same day and the Headmistress devoted most of her speech to extolling their virtues. I was grateful that I only got a small mention at the end for being someone who was good at listening.

The day was subdued. There was no end-of-term pantomime. Figgis hadn't felt like writing one and no one else had stepped into the breach. There was no drunken party and no one suggested retiring to the pub, so I sneaked out of the school having said quiet goodbyes to those closest to me: Figgis, Sharon Day, Beryl Smith, Perky Percy, Sean Carson, Pam Drabble.

Colin was the last person I said goodbye to. I found him slumped over the staffroom desk looking unshaven and very tired.

"Good working with you," I said, stuck for something to say.

"Was it?" he said. "I doubt that very much."

I didn't want to leave it like this so I reassured him that he had been great. My toes were curling in my shoes. He shrugged and with that I left, abandoning the moist, smoky fugginess of the Truss staffroom forever. Never again to walk in the mornings through derelict streets stuffed with litter and burnt-out cars. Never again to hear the squeals of pigs and baas of sheep in the strange city farm. Never again to see the grim spire of St Anthony's hovering darkly over the school. Never again to have a role in the Truss Book of Fate.

## EPILOGUE

The tale of what happened at Truss after I left is now the stuff of front-page news. In 2002 it was named as the most improved school in the country. Its results shot up from having about 5% of pupils achieving A-C GCSE grades to 70% pupils achieving this.

How did the school improve so much? Perhaps it was something to do with my leaving the school... or perhaps it was because the governors did manage to edge out the Headmistress and put someone more dynamic in the post. He set about improving school discipline and making the kids take more suitable courses. He knew how to play the statistics game and knew that there are certain vocational courses called GNVQs which count as GCSEs for statistical purposes but aren't examined by exams like GCSEs. Pupils can complete coursework modules in their chosen subjects and pick up good grades at the end of them.

But it mustn't be forgotten that Truss had something that very few inner-city schools have: a stable staff who had the respect of the kids. The new Head had a good base from which to start improving the school. I think this is the single most important factor in making a school successful: permanent, hard-working teachers. Many of the teachers who I knew at Truss ten years ago are still there.

One person who is not there is Colin. I bumped into Pam in Leystonstone High Road a few months after I started at Wickstead and she told me that he had been arrested. Apparently, he had been charged with sexually assaulting a few of the boys who he had taken to the rural studies centre in Wales.

"He was clever," she said with her lip trembling. "He never did it at his house when he took them there. He groomed them and then he did it, the bastard. God, if I ever see him again, I'll kill him!"

It was a chilly night and it was beginning to rain so I didn't talk to her long. I wasn't sure that I wanted to know every detail. At the time, I just wanted to concentrate upon my new job which was turning out to have its own unique challenges. I didn't want to think about Truss. I just wanted to move on.

Life back at my new "old" school was occupying most of my mind.

# How to be a Bad Birdwatcher
## To the greater glory of life
### Simon Barnes
1-904095-95-X

Look out of the window.
See a bird.
Enjoy it.
Congratulations. You are now a bad birdwatcher.

Anyone who has ever gazed up at the sky or stared out of
the window knows something about birds. In this funny,
inspiring, eye-opening book, Simon Barnes paints a
riveting picture of how bird-watching has framed his life
and can help us all to a better understanding of our place
on this planet.

    *How to be a bad birdwatcher* shows why birdwatching
is not the preserve of twitchers, but one of the simplest,
cheapest and  most rewarding pastimes around.

## "An ode to the wild world outside the kitchen window"
### Daily Telegraph